To Sue
Kind Regards
Peter T. Healey

ROUGH JUSTICE

Essex Murders, United Kingdom

PETER THOMAS HEALEY

Copyright © 2012 Peter Thomas Healey
All rights reserved.

ISBN: 146995186X
ISBN-13: 9781469951867

BRAINTREE AND WITHAM TIMES

Blyth's Meadow, Braintree, Essex CM7 6DN
Telephone 26501

November 24 1986

P Healey,
15 Bull Lane,
TIPTREE.

Dear Mr Healey,

I am sorry but I cannot help you with back copies of the Braintree and Witham Times. We simply do not have them. However, we do have filed bound copies or, for the later issues, microfilm files.

From 1929 to 1970 newspapers are at the Braintree office; From 1971 to 1977 they are on microfilm at the Colchester Editorial Library in Oriel House, North Hill; From 1978 to the present, copies of the microfilm are at Braintree.

Obviously you would have to go through them yourself to find what you want. I wish you the best of luck.

Yours sincerely,

RAY HARDISTY,
Braintree and Witham Times Editor.

ESSEX COUNTY NEWSPAPERS

Evening Gazette   Essex County Standard   Halstead Gazette & Advertiser   East Essex Gazette
Harwich & Manningtree Standard   Braintree & Witham Times   Maldon & Burnham Standard
Chelmsford Weekly News   Express Series
Company Registration No 850141 (England) Regd Office, 10 Culver Street West, Colchester, Essex CO1 1JE

The Book. Rough Justice

Complied by Peter T. Healey

Under The Freedom of Information Act, Rough Justice is the title of the case of Jeremy Bamber, an adopted child of a wealthy family. Read how rumours, mistakes and a catalogue of errors led to a man receiving several life sentences for murders that I feel he did not commit.

Webb Page

Book Disclaimer
The contents of this book have been scrutinized because of the seriousness, murder is a complicated issue. Any person, persons or places mentioned in this book are observations, not distortion – any similarity is not inferred. Except for the guilty. Legal watchdog.

Success is the planning effort and work towards a worthy cause.

(Author, (Peter T Healey) CPH

The Book. Rough Justice

Rough justice is not an issue to be taken lightly, especially if it involves someone receiving a Life sentence in Jail. It is awful enough if a person is guilty of the crimes. However it is compounded and even worse if an Individual is an innocent person. Why do such mistakes? Take place. Sometimes the murders are so shocking that a quick arrest is needed to stop the fear of the public. In the Jeremy Bamber case the first senior police officer in charge of this case did not feel sure that Jeremy Bamber committed the Murder of his adopted family. However things took a different turn when the officer in charge of the investigation was killed when having a weekend leave, he tragically fell from a ladder when painting part of his house. From then on the Jeremy Bamber case took on a new development. Much to the disaster for Jeremy Bamber's, I myself made a statement to the first police officer about things that I thought a Jury should hear at the trial of Jeremy Bamber's I was promised a copy of my statement. Yet I never did receive my copy. Also I know my evidence was never produced at Jeremy Bambers court Trial. I feel this evidence would of made the Jury uncertain has to give a guilty verdict against Jeremy Bamber for murders that I feel he did not commit.

You can tell a lie, A thousand Times and people will believe you

You can also Tell the Truth Once and No one Will Believe You?

The Book. Rough Justice.

Hi my reason for writing this book is because it is history it will also be a historic event, for future generations to read the shocking and dreadful events that happened whilst I actually worked in the Essex area. Especially in Coggeshall.

I was employed by Essex county council. At the Braintree Education Department as a Driver handyman for eleven years. These where a very happy period my bosses were excellent people, they knew how to relate to all the staff. Relations at Crossman house Braintree office were great.

During my employment I spent mainly five days a week working in the Coggeshall area for, eleven years. So it is understandable that I got to know a great deal about local life, and local people.

My job was variable, however I had to pick up children from outside of the Coggeshall area to take them to school and also return these children to their appointed pick up point. One of my journeys took me to Marks Hall just outside of Coggeshall. I had to pick up my children from a bungalow owned by farmer Jimmy Bell. Also Gardeners cottage, and the gamekeepers cottage. The parents of the child in the bungalow owned by Jimmy Bell had a second young son. The asked my employers if he could also be picked up by me on my school run. They moved a lot of people to get this permission for their son to travel on the bus. So imagine my surprise when on the Monday Morning no one was at the bungalow. It was hard for me to understand what on earth could be wrong. So I knocked on the door. Then I had a look through the window of the bungalow. Heard a voice say to me hey do you like hospital food. I replied not really. Then I noticed farmer Jimmy Bell holding a 22.rifle with a silencer. He said to me if I catch you looking through those windows again. I will put a bullet in your arse. Do you understand said yes I understand. Then I got back in my bus fast.

When the local doctors wife. Diane Jones got arrested for drink driving in her car. I noticed that her car was parked for a long time in the front garden of a local farmer's bungalow which was situated about 500 hundred yards from the main farm house, later Coggeshall became alive with rumours. When Diane Jones disappeared Press men and police were everywhere. 3 different local mothers told me quite clearly. That they would not look outside of Coggeshall for her killer.

Also a local farmer who had domestic problems was sent to prison for assaulting his wife. Later on he married again. One day I saw the farmers new wife walking alone and she was crying I asked if I could help. She said no. Please do not let Jimmy see me talking to you. She said he is going to hurt someone that I am fond of, I asked is there no one that you can talk to? About your worries. She then told me that she intended to discuss her problems with another farmer's wife Mrs Bamber, who was a religious person?

When working in Coggeshall I used to park my Bus in a Coggeshall car park. I used to keep racing pigeons so during my dinner time, I could keep my training results up to date. One day I was in my bus when a loud scattering effect happened. I was quite shocked. Parked next to me was a 4+4 land rover. Something had come off this vehicle and hit my bus. When I went to investigate a local Farmer standing in front of the land rover with a 22 rifle with a silencer on the end of the rifle. What the farmer had done was to throw a box of 22 bullets at the range rover. Then I heard the farmer say next time these bullets come at you they will come from this, he then waved his gun frantically. The people in the range rover next to me were Mr. and Mrs Bamber, who later on were murdered. They used to Bank in a Coggeshall Bank. The local farmer was saying Mr. Bamber could have helped him. When he the farmer was sent to prison for assaulting his wife.

I feel this information should have been

Heard at Jeremy Bambers trial. As I stated early on in this book that I have never received a copy of my statement. I often wonder what the reaction would have been if Jeremy Bambers sister had been found Guilty of these dreadful murders? Jeremy Bambers conviction for the family murders. Left more questions than answers. Not only must justice be done, justice should be seen to be done. However in this case. I feel an unjust view was concluded.

The local Doctors wife Diane Jones vanished, after leaving a local pub the Woolpack in Coggeshall. Also a couple and their children who were staying in a local farmers bungalow left without trace. Then later the local farmer used a farm tractor and trailer to clear his bungalow of carpets, curtains and furniture. I feel the police should have searched this bungalow. Because something mysterious happened there. Can you imagine sometime later. When I was told that a local farmer Jimmy Bell had travelled to Norfolk. To find his second wife. He then murdered his lovely wife. God bless her soul. Then he killed himself. He certainly was disturbed and a very angry person. He also had threatened Mr. Bamber. Who also was later found murdered with his family. I feel the police were very wrong not to connect these killings. I have a great deal of respect for the police. However mistakes can be made. One Essex police officer said to me personally about the Bamber killings. He said we got it wrong from the very start at the White House Farm scene of the Bamber murders.

One Point that I want to stress and mention is that all though Dr Jones was questioned and interviewed by Essex Police Dr Jones was never charged with any offence.

> So the question still remains. Who then did kill the local doctors wife Diane Jones?
>
> Dr Jones Life was turned upside down, with all the enquires. Yet many local residents have a good word for their doctor.
>
> Many more strange events happened to me whilst working in Coggeshall. As a result I bought a tree and had a statue of the Madonna Virgin Mary
>
> Carved in to a statue. Which I, gave to St Peters Church in Coggeshall.
>
> This was to appease the bad vibes that were happening in Coggeshall.

Letter to the Chief Constable [NOT PROTECTIVELY MARKED]

From: Sean O'Callaghan <Sean.O'Callaghan@essex.pnn.police.uk>
To: pthmidas@aol.com
Subject: Letter to the Chief Constable [NOT PROTECTIVELY MARKED]
Date: Mon, 23 Feb 2009 18:12

Classification: NOT PROTECTIVELY MARKED

Dear Mr Healey,

Rough Justice

Thank you for your letter dated the 18th February 2009.

The opportunity to comment on the contents of your intended publication 'Rough Justice' is acknowledged; however, Essex Police does not engage with opinions in such matters. Members of the public are entitled on matters of their choosing and therefore we would not seek to influence your project.

I can confirm that I am in safe receipt of the floppy disc that you enclosed with your letter. The content of the disc has not been viewed for the above reasons. Please could you kindly advise me if you would like the disc returned or disposed by my staff.

Once again thank you for taking the time to write to the Chief Constable.

Yours sincerely

Chief Inspector Sean O'Callaghan
Staff Officer to Chief Constable Roger Baker
Executive Support
Internal ext: 51016
Essex Police Number: 0300 333 4444
Direct Dial: 01245 452240
Fax 01245 452123
Website: www.essex.police.uk
Executive Support, PO Box 2, Spingfield, Chelmsford, CM2 6DA

To find out what is happening in your neighbourhood and all about your local neighbourhood policing team visit www.essex.police.uk/yourarea and enter your postcode

---

Privileged/Confidential Information and/or Copyright Material may be contained in this e-mail.

The information and Material is intended for the use of the intended addressee. If you are not the intended addressee, or the person responsible for delivering it to the intended addressee, you may not copy or deliver it to anyone else or use it in any unauthorised manner. To do so is prohibited and may be unlawful. If you receive this e-mail by mistake, advise the sender immediately by using the reply facility in your e-mail software.

Essex Police operate security software which can result in e-mails entering and leaving essex police being retained, opened and assessed to ensure compliance

ROUGH JUSTICE

S. PETER AD VINCULA, PARISH OF COGGESHALL WITH MARKSHALL
VICAR: The Reverend DAVID A. M. BEETON

The Vicarage,
4 Church Green,
Coggeshall,
Colchester,
CO6 1UD.

Telephone (0376) 61234

26th May 1986.

Dear Peter,

    I feel awful as I have taken so long to write to you and thank you for the carving of the Blessed Virgin. Legally I am not able to have a special Service yet as we have to apply for a faculty and this takes a considerable time.

    I will, however, carry out your request for prayers at a special Healing Service which will be held in the Lady Chapel on Wednesday 11th June at 8.00p.m. If you would like to join us for that Service you will be most welcome.

    Assuring you of my prayers.

        Yours sincerely,

        Fr David

X

SECRETARIAT OF STATE

FROM THE VATICAN, 17th February 1989

Dear Mr Healey,

I am directed to acknowledge the letter and the accompanying book which you sent to His Holiness Pope John Paul II, and I would assure you that the contents have been noted.

His Holiness will remember you in his prayers.

With good wishes, I remain

Yours sincerely,

Monsignor C. Sepe
Assessor

Mr Peter T. Healey
15 Bull Lane
TIPTREE
Essex
CO5 0BE

ROUGH JUSTICE

10 DOWNING STREET
LONDON SW1A 2AA

6 January 1989

Dear Mr Healey,

    I am writing on behalf of the Prime Minister to thank you for your recent letter and the enclosed book.

    I very much regret that, due to the sheer volume of requests which the Prime Minister receives for her signature, we have, reluctantly, had to introduce the rule that Mrs. Thatcher can only accede to these requests when they are connected with a charity.

    I can, however, send you a photograph of the Prime Minister which bears a facsimile of her signature and which, I hope, will go some way to alleviate your disappointment.

Yours sincerely,

P T Healey Esq.
15 Bull Lane
TIPTREE
Essex
CO5 0BE

Did I See a Vision

                                                    Is it a Sign
                                   Jeremy Bamber is Innocent
                                         Read This Book

Complied by Peter. T. Healey

Under the Freedom of Information act.
Rough Justice is the title of the case of Jeremy Bamber an adopted Child Of a Wealthy family. Read how rumours mistakes and a catalogue of erros led to a man receiving several life sentences. For Murders That I feel he did not commit.

Peter. T. Healey

ROUGH JUSTICE

Peter T Healey 18/2/2009
15 Bull Lane 01621-816921
Tiptree
Colchester
Essex pthmidas@aol.com
CO5 OBE Ref/Jeremy Bamber

Dear Chief Constable
I have recently read an article in the Colchester evening gazette, concerning a possible
Appeal against a conviction of murder concerning Jeremy Bamber.

I understand this case is being scrutinised by a serious crime review team. My reason for
Writing to you is because I have written a book titled Rough Justice
I did work for Essex County Council for eleven Years. I was employed as a driver handy man.
During my employment I was based in Coggeshall.as you may well record several years ago
Coggeshall was alive with crime and several well-documented murders.
My being based in Coggeshall at this period in time I new most of the people involved in this
Sensational episode
I did make a statement to the police concerning the local doctors wife Dian Jones.
I also made a statement to the officer in charge of the Jeremy Bamber case. A Welshman
He unfortunately died after an accident whilst painting his house.
My main reason for my letter is have you any objections to my book?
I did at the time of these murders write to the then Prime Minister Margaret Thatcher I also
Wrote to the Pope and the local vicar at Coggeshall Saint Peters church plus I spoke
To two members of parliament. Concerning my fears that an innocent man had been convicted
On several counts of murder.
I am not trying to create waves. I do not intend to make any money from this book I will donate
Any proceeds to a community watchdog concern

Kind regards Please find enclosed a floppy disc of most of my book

Peter T Healey

The Book. Rough Justice

Jeremy Bamber

Protestations of innocence continued for quarter of a century

■ Tears – Bamber with his girlfriend at the funeral in 1985

- August 7, 1985: The bodies of Nevill and June Bamber, their daughter Sheila Caffell and her twin sons Daniel and Nicholas are found at White House Farm, Tolleshunt D'Arcy. They had all died from gunshot wounds

- August 16, 1985: Bamber attends the funeral of his family with girlfriend Julie Mugford. She later tells police he had talked of hiring a hitman to kill his parents

- September 8, 1985: Bamber is arrested for murder but released after five days. He is later re-arrested as he arrives back in England from France

- October 28, 1986: Bamber stands trial at Chelmsford Crown Court and is convicted by the jury

- March 20, 1989: He loses his first appeal

- December, 2002: After a three-week hearing at the Court of Appeal, Bamber loses his second appeal, which centres on a flake of blood which may or may not have been from Sheila.

- May 30, 2004: Bamber's throat is cut by another inmate at Full Sutton Prison and he is taken to hospital for treatment

- May 16, 2008: Bamber is told he will die in jail after his life tariff is reviewed at the High Court. Mr Justice Tugendhat ruled the murders were so serious he should never be freed.

- February 12, 2009: Bamber launches a further attempt at securing a third appeal

- March 2009: He once again claims evidence has been discovered that should allow him to appeal. It is not granted

- July 2010: He is refused a six-month extension to carry out tests on evidence and awaits to hear if a new appeal will be allowed.

Hi, my reason for writing this book is because it is history. It will also be a historic event for future generations to read. The shocking and dreadful events that happened whilst I actually worked in the Essex area. Especially in Coggeshall.

I was employed by Essex county council, at the Braintree Education Department, as a driver handyman for eleven years. These were a very happy period, my bosses were excellent people, they knew how to relate to all the Staff. Relations at Crossman House, Braintree Office, were great.

During my employment I spent mainly five days a week working in the Coggeshall area, for eleven years. So it is understandable that I got to know a great deal about local life, and local people.

My job was variable, however, I had to pick up children from outside of the Coggeshall area to take them to school and also return these children to their appointed pick up point. One of my journeys took me to Marks Hall just outside of Coggeshall. I had to pick up children from a bungalow owned by farmer Jimmy Bell, also from Gardeners Cottage, and Gamekeepers Cottage. The parents of the child in the bungalow owned by Jimmy Bell had a second young son. They asked my employers if he could also be picked up by me on my school run. They moved a lot of people to get this permission for their son to travel on the bus. So imagine my surprise when on the Monday morning when no one was at the bungalow. It was hard for me to understand what on earth could be wrong. So I knocked on the door. Then I had a look through the window of the bungalow. I heard a voice say to me "hey, do you like hospital food?" I replied, "Not really". Then I noticed farmer Jimmy Bell holding a .22 rifle with a silencer. He said to me "If I catch you looking through those windows again, I will put a bullet in your arse. Do you understand?" I said "Yes I understand" Then I got back in my bus Fast.

True sensational events that shocked an English community.

Mysterious happenings, psychic secrets, murder and mystery, witchcraft rituals.

The Jeremy Bamber Rough Justice Story.

There is enough in the world,
For the world's needs,
Yet there is not enough,
For the world's greed's.

Yet if everyone cared enough,
And everyone shared enough,
Then maybe everyone would
Have enough?

The Town of Coggeshall with a history of witchcraft and many more strange stories. Coggeshall is now a mixture of the old and the new, however, mystery is not far away. Did the ancient order of the knights of St John, the Templars, bring the Holy Grail to Coggeshall during their campaign to the Holy Land?

England's oldest recorded town is about 10 miles away. Queen Bodacea or Bodica, burnt most of Colchester to the ground according to historians. Coggeshall, Colchester and indeed all of Essex is well worth a visit.

"Coggeshall".

The once very important Town of Coggeshall, in Essex, England, is not all about antiques and murders. There is a great charm and history. Not far away in the village of Messing is the history of the family tree of the American Presidents. The Bush family have been found and recorded.

CHAPTER ONE

"The House," Tiptree: The Beginning

I suppose the purpose of writing a book is to get something off your chest or to clear the air. The purpose of buying a book may be varied. The reason I have written this book is a mixture of reasons to clear my mind to relate my experiences to satisfy an urge to tell the tale as I have witnessed it. Sometimes it have been very, very disturbing to say the least, the path my life has led. For me to go into detail about the supernatural is not my intension, neither have I full knowledge of the supernatural? I do feel there is another dimension to life other than physical. I also feel there will be a big breakthrough soon on this subject. Whether they actually find the answer is a different matter. I do not want to mislead readers to think that I search for demons or even practice – I do not.

Most of my tales and experiences have happened naturally. I moved to this house in Essex after leaving the North of England. I have lived at the house in Tiptree for the past 14 years. It has been a very enlightening experience. The house where I live is an old Essex-type semi-detached with the Essex boarding on the front; it is joined to next door. They started as a pair of cottages. Although they started as two-bedroom houses, they have both been extensively modernized. A strange feature this, although my wife sold next door, no one has lived there for about 10 years. Strange. My first visit to Tiptree, in Essex, was one Saturday. I was living in Braintree at the time and a friend of mine asked me if I would like to go to Tiptree to pick some strawberries. Tiptree is famous for its jam factory which was started by the Wilkin family in the last century. As I say, this was my first visit to Tiptree. After picking strawberries, we went to the local pub, The Ship Inn. It was quite colourful as there were students from universities from all over the world, who were on their vacation and living on the camps provided by the strawberry growers. It was a semi-paid holiday for them. Whilst in The Shipp Inn I got talking to a gentleman casually at the bar, he seemed to be able to communicate with me with his mind without actually talking, although we did not have a conversation. I enjoyed my first visit to Tiptree, it was, after all, a great changed from where I had been living. Three years later I went back to Tiptree to the house where I have lived for the last 14 years.

My wife lived in the house a few years longer than me. She had previously married. Two years earlier she had been involved in a very bad car accident in France whilst on holiday. Her late husband was killed by the accident. My wife received dreadful injuries and has now greatly recovered her health which is a miracle really, as it was touch and go to decide to amputate her badly injured leg. The gentleman I spoke to in The Ship at Tiptree on my first visit there was my wife's husband, who later was killed in France. He was a retired RAF sergeant; he had travelled all over the world and had been educated in the very top schools in India.

My wife rarely talks about the accident, although we have had some conversations on the subject. She did say her late husband had told her he thought something was going to happen to him, but he did not know exactly, but he made her promise that if he died he would try everything possible to get in contact with her. My wife said such conversation like this made her ill, especially when they had young children to care for.

The children are now adult, and the girls have married. I have visited the grave of her late husband in France several times; we did take the youngest child with us on one occasion. The grave is in a little village called Ardes, about 10 miles from Calais. The reason I tell you this part of the story is because, before the accident everyone lived in this house in Tiptree. I don't wish to enlarge too fully on other things which took place in this house, as it may be a bit misleading. This story did not happen overnight, it took about 15y years. Every incident seemed strange. But when you look back it has a pattern and I believe a meaning and probably a message.

One story I feel I must tell you concerning this house is, next-door-but-next is the vicar's house/ One evening about 5:30 there was knock on our door. I went to see who it was and when I opened the door there was a lady there. She said "I do not wish to disturb you, I have seen flames coming from next door". At this time both houses were owned by us. I thought workmen renovating next door had left a heater on. A newspaper boy also reported seeing these flames. I got the key and went next door, I looked all round but I could find no signs of flames or burn marks or fire. The Reverend Ruffle lived next door; he also saw these flames, as it was most unusual to other people I told the Reverend Ruffle and his wife not to worry too much as the Holy Ghost had come to visit e- strange coincidence, but true.

Most things that happen can normally be explained. But sometimes events that take place have no reasonable explanation as to why they happen. On several occasions unusual things have taken place which have left me completely baffled. I have been told sometimes spirits can remain earthbound until the work they have to do on earth is finished. This is one explanation. But I suppose as there is little evidence to explain otherwise, this theory is often accepted.

The once very important Town Of Coggeshall, In Essex, England

Is not all about antiques and Murders
There is a great charm and a history not far away is the village of messing history of the family tree of The American Presidents Of Americas. Bush family have been found and recorded.

Coggeshall's unique charm.

It Is Not All Antiques

When people read or hear tales and stories of good luck or misfortune, they tend to say "Cor, they are lucky" or "gee that's bad news". What exactly is luck? It is a very difficult thing to define. Often people seem to possess a great deal of luck, others not so lucky. So we are left with the question of what is luck? Luck, in my opinion, is when something nice happens. In a great deal of life's mysteries, often things run together or oppose each other, life North and South, positive and negative, life and death, love and hate, repentance or vengeance. I could name a lot more. All I am trying to formulate in the reader's mind is that luck has no equals – you have it or you do not, and rarely does it stay with a person forever. Quite often people have a fair share of luck – other people chase luck. It is a true saying you will not win if you don't enter; is it luck if you win, or is it pure chance? Chance is not luck but sometimes luck and chance so run together. Although they are separate in their own entirety: your last chance does not mean it's the end of your luck.

But you cannot actually see the results of luck. Such as wealth, property, and prosperity, hardly industrious labour, is not luck, it is hard work and perseverance. Laziness and idleness is not bad luck, it is lack of effort, No one is going to knock on your door and give you a fortune or thriving business; you have to make the effort. Education does not give you common sense; common sense is about the greatest gift that any living person or creature can have. There are people who, because of illness or injuries, cannot use the gift of common sense. Common sense goes a long way in creating or attracting luck, so try and improve your own common sense and you could be on the road to good luck. Common sense is very important if you go into your local club or pub and drink too much, and then drive your car; if you are stopped by the police, this is not bad luck; it is a misuse of common sense.

If you buy a raffle ticket and win a prize this is chance and luck. If you make good decisions and achieve good results, this is logical thinking. If you mix with villains, the chances are you are liable in the future to come across the law.

If you are a chef, and you create or prepare beautiful meals, you are selective in your choice of ingredients; the wrong choice can have the result of spoiling your meal, even once the ingredients are well mixed, they still have to be cooked, but most important the meal has to be served well. Different people, different families and different countries have their own special menus and their own way of preparing and serving meals, so common sense and good menu, well prepared and well served will bring satisfying results. This is not chance nor luck, but common sense.

So what you have read it is common sense to have a menu for your mind, the mind menu must have carefully selected ingredients. The ingredients must be prepared, approved and used well in the right company. If you make up your own "mind recipe", if it is a success, the chances are luck will come your way. Chance and luck often run together. Each person has their own individual appetite, so it is best for each person or individual to create their own recipe.

This private menu should be memorised, practiced and digested, there are many varieties, so chose one to suit your mind and energize your mind. The strengths from these practices are amazing in their benefits.

It must be fully understood my associated with any form of witchcraft came about after I found the Coggeshall Urn and other items in the back of the builder's truck in Coggeshall.

Since most of these events happened I have moved houses completely and I am very pleased to say that all disturbances whether spiritual, psychic, imagination or otherwise have left me completely. I am now at peace with the cosmos. I am no longer disturbed by poltergeists.

Mind Power

Magical powers are an extension of the powers of your mind, these powers are available for most people's use, but the majority of people never use the powers which are available to them. It is just as well really, because without any doubt the mind is in constant touch with the forces of nature. Nature has its own natural forces, you cannot harness nature. Nature has a plan of its own, you cannot tell nature what to do. But you can use useful practices to get help in your quest for whatever it is your wish to achieve or obtain. I myself have used several different methods for attracting good fortune, good health and strength, and protection from forces and circumstances which I have been in.

Quite often I have found it to be in my experience that when you know you can't win, and there is the possibility of losing, you have to compromise. I believe compromise is one of the greatest escape exits available to mankind. It is a good lesson to learn to compromise, because it can useful in all types of situations, after all, we cannot all be right. So from today, if a situation arises which is a bit "iffy", always remember a compromise is a terrific solution to being about a sensible end to whatever the problem may be.

The mind like the body has to work to the best advantage of the person or body within its control. After all, it is through the influence of the mind. Thought runs the body, so it would be a good thing to think good of most people; this is useful use of good mind power. To get good results, I feel you have to have a certain amount of discipline. Discipline is a recipe of a code of conduct to formulate mind power. Mind power is like an electrical current: it can be switched on – do not waste the power. It is a free agent and a very important power. It is difficult to really obtain complete power of one's own mind, because we either start too late to learn to programme our mind, after all the mind is a very good equivalent of an astonishing computer. Thoughts are always flowing through the mind's circuits. To achieve success with mind power, you have to use a certain amount of mind discipline. Discipline does not come easy, you have, as I've stated, got to concentrate. First concentrate on ridding yourself of every kind of thought and all disturbances, clear your minds enagrams – an enagram is a mental thought pattern. Once your mind is satisfactory clear, form a mental enagram of the desired item you wish to achieve, say to yourself, "this is what I want, I need this, this is what I am going to achieve". Start your concentration by closing your eyes, have very little disturbances, after concentrating your thoughts, as long as possible, open your eyes slowly. Do not ask for too much to begin with. Start by visualizing peaceful surroundings, like home, family health. When you achieve these needs, progress to your wildest dreams. If your doubt you lose; no doubts are needed for success. Life's life force is always there. It is true what you sow you will reap. Use your thoughts to enter the creative life computer. There is no difference to using your mind thoughts to order things than to order a pint of beer. So start today: relax and discipline your mind to order life's pleasures; remember, start small, take your time and concentrate. Good luck.

Useful Information

It is very, very important that whenever you decide to use mind power, to learn to relax properly. I myself find it a great comfort to relax and clear my mind of all the irritations and let the clear thoughts wash my brain. Thoughts have wings. All types of mind disturbances can be removed and replaced by energy, given cleansing thoughts. Sometimes it can be difficult to find the time, or pace to perform or relax to do your mind exercises. I have often isolated myself completely and just went to bed, not to ask for anything, but just to relax. Before you go to sleep is a good time to clear your mind of irritations – also early morning. If you clear your mind at night, you should have a clear mind in the morning. It is ill advised to purchase a mind power book, and immediately you have to read to try to obtain the impossible. It is good advice to clear one's mind, bit by bit, piece by piece. It can be done and it has to be done to progress. When people realise or find out your are interested in mind power, you nearly always get asked "Do you know all about black arts and voodoo?" I know tell people this is not always mind power. Black arts, voodoo and other cults can be very dangerous indeed. I myself now concentrate on the white side of magic. This side can give you great pleasure from your learning, you do not have to be a witch or belong to a coven to practice the white arts. I get by without an altar, but if it pleases you, this is a general of what some altars consist of. This is only a practical description. I know some altars have priceless items attached to them, others are just as basic as when Abraham was alive.

The sitting, or placing of your altar, or your table, or even shrine, is of importance. You can be out of line with the cosmic energies to influence your rituals. No sacrifices are needed for white magic. I feel the best results can be obtained so the altar or place of sanctity or worship should face the rising sun, so that it always rises before you.

The size of any altar is up to the individual. A white cloth is popular, coloured table mats can be used for various requests. Your zodiac candle is needed; yellow for money, also green. A charcoal intense burner is required. Oils are used, herbs, antacid resin, you can light perfumed joss sticks. Your robe or belt, a skull or pendant, a bell chalice offering plate. I use fruit, your blessed altar knife, goblet or chalice, your altar candles to the back of the altar, your knife blade pointing to the rising sun. a glass of water should be there, one with salt, one glass of clear water.

Red wine, one large standard white candle for the presence of power. A coloured candle to represent the request, and you can if you wish use just white candles. Anoint the large white candle with a perfume of your choice, fill your incense burner with your favourite odour, light your large candle, stand before it, with the small candle in your hand, look into the flames of the large candle and say "energy of the flames of fire, grant the wish I desire". Name your wish, then light the small candle from the flame of the large candle. It is always best to say a cleansing prayer before all ceremonies. You can make up your own, it is also required to offer thanks in words, and also sprinkle drops of salt water all around. Now use your incense burner for contact, your offertory plate should a written request. Burn you request, and say "Oh Almighty, mighty power help me at this altar, before you is my request, from your servant, I thank thee" Then drink your wine.

Finish of saying something like, "I attract unto myself the powers of good fortune" try to use the same time of day or night for ritual request. It does work; I know, because I have actually done this. It is sensible to think lucky. When you do this it becomes a habit, when it becomes habit, it generally becomes natural; it joins the cosmic rhythm waves which achieves luck.

Certain items or objects tend to bring about good luck or fortune. It is a good thing to have a good charm, or object somewhere safe, where it can be radiate luck waves. Sometimes the truth is very hard to understand, sometimes

Useful Information

if you tell the truth people fail to believe you – on the other hand, if you tell lies, the chances are you could be believed. For instance you could tell lies and people could believe you, and you could tell them "cor, that was a bit of luck". Well, was it?

The Coggeshall Urn (Fonte)

Some time ago I was going through a difficult stage of my life, things were not really bad, but things were not exactly right. I seemed to be going one step forward and ten steps back. I had a constant unsettled feeling, I thought it was my conscience because I had not been going to church. So for several weeks I went regularly to church. I had confession, still I had this uneasy feeling.

At this time I was working five days a week in Coggeshall, Essex. I kept racing pigeons and lived in Tiptree. A friend of mine who also lived in Tiptree, who kept pigeons, asked him if I would take him in my car to train our pigeons, as the pigeons were only young and just beginning to learn their future. It was a lovely evening so we decided to take our pigeons to Coggeshall, about seven miles away. We decided we would let the pigeons go on the car park of a pub called 'The Woolpack' in Coggeshall. I let the pigeons go and my friend I was with brought me a pint of beer. When we let the pigeons go, some workmen saw them fly away, and they asked me where they were flying to. I said "To Tiptree". We got talking to these workmen, who had a small lorry full of rubble. They told us they were pulling down a very old building in Coggeshall. One of the workmen said they had found full size black cat. Behind the wall of one of the bedrooms, a few old cloths, clay and wooden dolls. I went to have a look on the lorry; there I saw a full size cat, the dolls and a little metal urn. I asked the workmen if I could have the dirty old urn. He said "Yes, you can have the cat as well if you want". I said, "No thanks", we had a good laugh and a discussion on witchcraft, and then we said goodbye.

We went home to Tiptree, I dropped my friend at his home, and I also went home and out my pigeon baskets into my shed.

I looked in my pigeon loft, none of my young pigeons which I had let go at 'The Woolpack' at Coggeshall had returned. Next evening I went to my friend's home, none of his pigeons had returned. Between us we lost about £600 worth of young pigeons. The following Saturday I went to 'The Ship Inn' at Tiptree for a pint of beer. One of my friends asked about my young pigeons.

I told him about my trip to Coggeshall, and that none of the pigeons had returned. I told him about the builders pulling down the old house in Coggeshall, and about the cat and the dolls and the urn. They had a good laugh. I told them the urn was still in my car. A lady in @The Ship' asked if she could see the urn, so I went to get it.

It proved quite interesting, there were some words on the bottom of the urn, and it was very dirty, the neck of the urn was quite small, but it was a bit larger around the middle. However, it was decided that one of the words on the bottom of the urn was "witch". When you actually shook the urn, or Fonte, it had a rattle. I thought a piece of plaster had got inside. However, after a while, and a difficult struggle, I managed to get out a piece of parchment, dirty and stained with a drop of red wax on it. After straightening it out, you could read:

Keep me safe, anoint me well,
I will be your wishing well
What you need, what you want
Will come from the blessing of this Fonte.
ZARRUSA ZARRUSA
ACCLAMI LIZA

The Fonte, or urn has numerous markings on it. I thought it was probably in the wall to rid evil spirits. Other local people told me this was a custom years ago. Sometimes strange thins occurred when they were disturbed. However, that morning in 'The Ship' there was a big notice advertising a national competition, to be organized by Trumens Brewery. The prize was a holiday for two in Monte Carlo: also the licensee of the winning nominated pub would also win a holiday for two in Monte Carlo.

The Coggeshall Urn (Fonte)

The competition was on the back of a beer mat. Nominate and English pub and then give reasons why you thought your nominated pub should win. Well, one of my friends said, why don't you try your newly found urn, or Fonte? So I decided I would. A customer out a couple of drops of perfume in the urn and I place the urn on the beer mat. I later filled in the details and sent the beer mat away for the competition. That same evening I went to the local football club dinner and dance; during the evening a competition was held.

A very large bottle of whisky was places on the floor; competitors had to roll or slide ten pence pieces towards the bottle. I placed the urn behind the bottle, threw the ten pence pieces towards the bottle, two hit the bottle and one stopped immediately in front of the bottle.

Many people tried for over half an hour to beat my ten pence piece, but they could not. I won the bottle of whisky. I went back to my table in the club; a lady was selling raffle tickets. I brought 50 pence worth. I put the raffle tickets in the urn, there were three different colours, hundreds were sold. The first raffle ticket drawn was mine.

The following day my young pigeons came back, the ones which were lost form Coggeshall. I went to visit my friend to see if any of his pigeons had returned; they had not. The next week young bird racing started again, I was 1st Club. The week after I was 1st Club again and the third week I was 1,2,3 Club.

That season I won many prizes including first in three young bird race averages. The lowest winning velocity, the longest young bird race, and the young bird averages. My friend never did get his pigeons back from Coggeshall. He turned his loft into a garden shed and gave me his baskets and pigeon clock.

I still think of that cat that night at the Woolpack Inn at Coggeshall. Some people say the pigeons were spooked. I later learned that the cat was bricked back up again at the property in Coggeshall, because some strange events had disturbing influences on certain people.

Shortly after this incident I had decided a holiday was out of the question, as I decided to knock two bedrooms at my house into one, and have one door bricked up and the ceilings done, which I did as my friend was plastering the walls. He put some cladding underneath to soundproof the walls. As he did so it reminded me of the cat at Coggeshall. I told my friend about the cat. While I was telling him the tale, there was knock on the door. It was the postman with a letter. When I opened it, it said "Congratulations – you have been chosen as the lucky winner of our Monte Carlo holiday competition". Was this chance, coincidence, luck or mind power extraordinaire?

Sometime previously I went to a silver wedding at the "Barn" restaurant, Braintree. This Barn restaurant was the scene of a murder. The owner, during our meal, gave us a cake as a present and a bottle of champagne for the silver wedding couple. The owner was Mr. Bob Patience. The place was lovely, with thousands of pounds worth of antiques. During our conversation, he said he had achieved most things through mind power and not through physical strength.

Some years later, whilst at a church auction I brought a beautiful five-foot brass standard lamp, with markings on it. It was made in India and was reputed to have come from a mystic's house. The urn I found in Coggeshall had similar markings. After buying the lamp for £40, when I got to Tiptree. I decided to have lunch in a local pub. Whilst in there Bob Patience came in (the owner of the Barn) we discussed various subjects and I told him of the standard lamp, which I had brought. He asked to see it.

I said yes and he offered me £150 for the lamp, providing I brought his lunch. I finished up taking £140 for the lamp. Mr. Patience gave me his card, as he said he was not always successful, but he certainly a great believer in mind power. But he did say certain antique objects had some bad influences. I won't go into what he specified, but he brought, sold and exchanged antiques all over the world, one of his main sources being Coggeshall, Essex.

You may notice in my writing the work Coggeshall crops up regularly. I will give an explanation of this later.

Later the Barn restaurant, motel and all its antiques were sold, now Mr. Patience is no longer alive, but he left an everlasting impression on me for the wellbeing of mind power – he died a very wealthy man.

My Coggeshall urn has brought me luck in almost everything: raffles, football pools, lotteries, bingo, 100 Club, it has also helped others to win.

Coggeshall

Coggeshall is a very small town, no bigger than some villages. It is situated between Braintree and Colchester. It is clean, olde worlde type of place, there are new estates – it has a history.

It is to believed to be one of the very oldest towns in England. It had links with the wool trade. It has several churches, the oldest being St Peter's. There is no real industry. It is surrounded by countryside and farmland, most people commuting to work elsewhere. At the moment there are a large number of antique shops. Years ago you could easily visualise strange happenings.

Essex has a strong link with witchcraft, with trials held in Colchester and Chelmsford Assizes, many witches put to death.

The devil is supposed to of appeared at Barn Hall, Tolleshunt Knights, not far away. A local once told me years ago, a local man looked into the river and saw the reflection of the moon and thought it was a giant cheese. He dived into the river to get the cheese to share with his friend. All he got was a ribbing.

My reason for including quite a lot about Coggeshall is because recently there have been strange happenings, some quite horrific, and it has all or most of it happened during the time I have worked in this area – which brings me back to mind power.

I mentioned the Barn Restaurant and Bob Patience earlier, because Braintree is not far away. Mrs Patience was murdered there. I feel there is a link somewhere and I have been guided to write about it.

These stories are for demonstration purposes only and are not meant as a detective enquiry or witch hunt.

I feel these people were once successful with mind power, but later abused the power. Genius and inspirations are rare – mind power can be achieved and be very successful, if used properly. At the moment I have read that there is a curse on Coggeshall, also that it is on lay, where lay lines cross.

Recently there has been the tragic case of the local doctor's wife, Diane Jones, who after an evening out at the Woolpack Inn in Coggeshall, much the worse for drink, she was taken to her home in Coggeshall.

Months later she was found murdered, her badly decomposed body being near Ipswich. He husband took her home, sometime later she walked out of the house, never to be seen alive again.

As I know Coggeshall and the Woolpack Inn, it is about four minutes from her home. If a person was too drunk to walk home, it seems strange how she could walk away later that night. Drink makes people do strange things.

Her husband, Dr. Robert Jones, never reported her missing for several days.

Going back to Diane Jones, earlier one Saturday morning I was taking my wife's mother home to Chelmsford when a car same along the A12, going the wrong way. It was Diane Jones, she was drunk and later breathalysed, and had to go to Witham Court, where she lost he licence.

Another time some people I know were having a Bonfire Party. While they were in the garden, Diane Jones walked into their house, opened the drinks cupboard and helped herself. These people were really surprised to see her, as she was not invited or a personal friend, so her behaviour pattern was unpredictable.

I used to visit a house just outside Coggeshall. It was a bungalow really and owned by a Coggeshall farmer, Mr. Bell, who recently murdered his second wife and then killed himself. When I used to visit the house, Mr. Bell was still married to his first wife. He got six months imprisonment for abuse to his wife.

Mr. Bell was later divorced and married his second wife. The bungalow where I had to go was frequented by American servicemen. It has been stated that Diane Jones was pregnant. You can draw your own conclusions; one thing is for certain – she was found near an American airbase. Dr. Jones was interviewed but never charged or stood trial.

Another tragic case was when Coggeshall millionaire Wilfred Bull shot his wife dead in Coggeshall. My reason for mentioning these cases is because I do not think a curse exists on Coggeshall and I do not think it has anything to do with lay lines.

It is a bit of everything: greed, lust, over-indulging. I feel the trouble may be linked to the antique trade. Before Diane Jones left her husband, she lived temporarily in Goldhanger, on the coast of Essex.

Some years ago "Italian Tony" was murdered in a gaming place whilst playing a one-armed bandit. Italian Tony some years earlier had been blamed for killing a well-known Londoner's brother. Just recently there was the horrific massacre of an Essex family – the Bamber case.

Mr. Bamber was an Essex magistrate. Strange coincidence, but true. Italian Tony lived in the Goldhanger area of Essex.

This has all the hallmarks of a contract killing with underworld Mafia links.

Spiritualism

I have a strong belief in spiritualism. I feel a great deal is still yet unknown. I have attended about six different spiritualist churches. I have always found the people to be friendly, sympathetic and helpful. Almost every time I visited a church the medium told me that I am psychic, and that I should develop into a medium.

Some of the messages are very accurate, and could only have been passed on my one deceased person, because it would have been impossible for a living person to know, because I am a stranger to Essex. So I would say I am a believer. I hope, also, a Christian.

I have had many, many messages from the Other Side: too many to be a figment of my imagination. I feel Princess Grace of Monaco contacted me, as did Elvis Presley and Doris Stokes, who was very upset about Paul Daniel's remarks about her. She said he would be taught different one day. The force that guides his tongue also guides his hands.

Several things have happened to me in the past that makes it so obvious that there is a guiding force for mankind.

What Bob Geldof does should be done by all states of the world. What Gorbachev has offered is a step towards unity of the world.

But what God has promised is salvation for all souls of all mankind.

Coggeshall Toilets Scandal

Coggeshall first hit the headlines in March, 1978, when the town's public toilets were revealed as a notorious meeting place for homosexuals.

Fourteen, among them company directors and other business people, were later convicted of indecency offences.

The dreadful trail of death in Coggeshall, a sleepy town best known for its string of antique shops, began five years ago in July, 1983, when the enigmatic wife of the village doctor disappeared.

Sex perverts, queers, gays, transvestites, steamers from all parts of East Anglian used to be attracted to Coggeshall market toilets. One man was alleged to have been charged £20 to have sex with a beautiful blonde haired rubber doll. Apparently he was very drunk and went berserk.

When questioned, he said "I gave her kiss, a love bite on the neck and she farted and flew out of the door!"

It must be stated that these people who frequented the Coggeshall toilets were not all local people, but visitors. Coggeshall is a very nice people and well worth a visit.

The Woolpack

The Woolpack Inn, Coggeshall, is an olde worlde type of inn with plenty of Oak beams. It looks old and is built as though it has come out of a history book. People tell me that food is excellent.

I feel it has an atmosphere all of its own. The two occasions when I actually had a drink there I felt cold and chilled and ill-at-ease. It is only a few yards from St. Peter's Church. A perfect setting, in years gone by, for a celebration drink after a wedding, or condolence after a funeral.

I feel a voice from the past shouting out to me "Let me out, let me out!" The psychic awareness or paranormal could be exorcised with good results around this area of Coggeshall.

It is well worth a visit.

Diane Jones Murder

The Diane Jones disappearance set the town of Coggeshall alive. Newspapermen, TV crews to there in great numbers, their camera equipment seemed to be everywhere. The police had a mobile caravan special police station in Coggeshall for months. Police enquiries were estimate at over a million pounds. Some of the bypass was dug up and Dr. Jones' house gate was removed.

Coggeshall is a very small place, so over a period of time you tend to have innocent contact with a great many people. It seemed to me to be strange that after she disappeared, a great number of unpleasant stories appeared. Had she been alive, I think a few people would have faced libel cases.

Dr. Jones ex-wife is now married to a local antique dealer, Mr. John Smith.

All these people were interviewed about Diane Jones' disappearances. After leaving the Woolpack and going home, Diane Jones' mind was not her own through drink – Diane Jones disappeared. Most people I have spoken to speak highly of Dr. Jones, but his behaviour had been rather unpredictable. His experience must have been living hell.

Dr. Jones has been back by health watchdogs following complaints from some of his patients. The Mid Essex Community Health Council received complaints from five of Dr. Jones' patients. The complaints were reported to the Council by one of its members who lived in the town. However, the Council backed Dr. Jones and dismissed the complaints. The Council's secretary said that the only advice they could offer was that if people felt they could no longer go to Dr. Jones, they should change their doctor. The Family Practitioner Committee would ensure they were attached to another GP's practice if that was what they wanted. A receptionist at Dr. Jones' practice said she did not want to discuss the matter.

Diane Jones' killer is still at large. Police have never closed the file on the woman whose decomposing body was found only yards from the busy main road in Suffolk, three months after she went missing. She had been brutally battered to death – her skull was smashed by four blows from a weapon thought to be a roof tiler's hammer – and dumped in woodland near the village of Brightwell.

The 35 year old wife of flamboyant Dr Jones was last seen alive after drinking with her husband at the Woolpack Inn on July 23rd 1983 – she went off into the night and was never seen again. Dr. Jones was quizzed days after the disappearance, but no charges were ever bought.

The very busy main road is only a few steps from Dr Jones' home. A drunken woman would be very easy prey for the many people who used that busy section of the road. The rights and wrongs of this case are a mystery.

ROUGH JUSTICE

The Message in the ancient vase.
Many schemes, ideas, plans, and medals potions. Statues and prayers
Incantations, candle burning, witchcraft, oils, have been used to bring
About. Luck and good fortune, including fire and holy water.
However I feel the benefit of the pyramid. Scroll that I found inside
An old ancient vase. In the ancient town in Coggeshall. In Essex has been
Influential in bringing good changes and vibes into my life than any
Other known mystical way that brings about good fortune.

The piece of parchment read, annoint me well I will be your wishing well
Not what you want. But what you need. Will come true. With the blessing
Of this deed, arrusa arussa calma- cama carn.

The pyramid message is

```
         I
         Me
         Will
         Find
         Health
         Wealth
        Strength
        Happiness
        Prosperity
       Enlightment
      AcclaimiLiza
      ZarussaZarussa
```

The Coggeshall Urn

The Woolpack inn, Coggeshall
The last place Diane Jones was
Seen alive?

Inquest opens into double shootings

AN inquest into the violent deaths of wealthy Coggeshall farmer James Bell and his young wife Augusta was opened on Monday.

Coroner for Diss, Norfolk, Ernest Clark, recorded that the bodies of Mr Bell, 50, and his 22-year-old wife had been identified by Mrs Bell's stepfather Michael Goodier of Grove Cottages, Upper Billingford, Norfolk.

Mr Goodier made the identification on Wednesday after the bodies of Mr and Mrs Bell were discovered by police.

Mr Bell blasted his wife to death and then turned the gun on himself, after the couple had a furious row at Grove Cottages.

Mr Bell, of Bouchiers Farm, Coggeshall, had travelled to Norfolk to see his estranged wife, who was staying with her mother.

No details of the cause of the deaths were given at the inquest.

The inquest was adjourned until September 2, when it will be reopened at Diss Corn Hall.

Police had found the bodies of Mr Bell and his estranged wife Augusta, 22, side-by-side in her mother's home.

Mrs Bell's mother, Mrs Sally Goodiers, had taken her daughter's 18-month-old child, Victoria, out of the cottage as a fierce row developed between the couple.

Mrs Goodiers has now taken Victoria to hide out with relatives in Suffolk.

Armed police broke into the cottage after a four-hour siege. Three shots had been fired as Mrs Goodiers ran from her home.

Police found a shotgun near the bodies.

It is believed that Mrs Bell had walked out of their home in Bouchiers Grange, Coggeshall, six weeks ago, taking her daughter with her.

Norfolk police said they were not looking for anyone else in connection with the shooting.

Police confirmed that no one else was in the house at the time of the killing.

A BABY girl was snatched to safety minutes before her father went berserk with a shotgun and blasted her mother to death.

Millionaire Coggeshall farmer James Bell, 50, then turned the gun on himself at a secluded cottage in a Norfolk village.

Police found the bodies of Bell and his estranged wife Augusta, 22, side-by-side in her mother's home in Upper Billingford yesterday afternoon.

It was revealed today that Mrs Bell's mother, Sally Goodiers, had taken her daughter's 18-month-old child, Victoria, out of the cottage as a fierce row developed between the couple.

Armed police later broke into the cottage after a four-hour siege.

Three shots had been fired as Mrs Goodiers ran from her home.

BLAZING

Police found a shotgun near the bodies.

It is believed that Mrs Bell had walked out of their home at Bouchiers Grange, Coggeshall, six weeks ago, taking her daughter with her.

Bell turned up at the house unexpectedly, and after a blazing row the shooting took place.

Bell married Augusta in 1982, after serving a six-month prison sentence for a bizarre attack on his first wife Janet. He put her through a humiliating ordeal for allegedly having an affair with another man.

Today one of Bell's close friends in Coggeshall said: "I would be very surprised if he had shot himself.

"I am not surprised that he lost his temper but I don't believe he would have turned the gun on himself."

He confirmed that he used to meet Bell in local pubs for heavy drinking sessions.

"He was very popular. He was a man's man and lots of fun."

Norfolk police said they were not looking for anyone else in connection with the shooting.

Police confirmed that no one else was in the house at the time of the killings.

Mrs Goodiers and 18-month-old Victoria were today staying with relatives

COGGESHALL, the colourful market town which has had more than its share of scandal and intrigue, is in the headlines again.

Another of its characters, some would say eccentrics, is involved in murder — the third bizarre killing in as many years.

Mr. Bell – Coggeshall

Coggeshall, the colourful market town which has had its fair share of scandal and intrigue, is in the headlines again. Another of its characters, some would say eccentrics, is involved in murder – the third bizarre killing in as many years.

A baby girl was snatched to safety minutes before her father went berserk with a shotgun and blasted her mother to death. Millionaire Coggeshall farmer James Bell, 50, then turned the gun on himself at a secluded cottage in a Norfolk village. Police found the bodies of Bell and his estranged wife Augusta, 22, side by side in her mother's home in Upper Billingford.

It was revealed that Mrs Bell's mother, Sally Goodiers, had taken her daughter's 18 month old daughter, Victoria, out of the cottage as a fierce row developed between the couple. Armed police later broke into the cottage after a four siege. Three shots had been fired as Mr. Goodiers ran from her home.

Police found a shotgun near the bodies. It is believed that Mrs Bell had walked out of their home at Bouchiers Grange, Coggeshall, six weeks previously, taking her daughter with her. Bell turned up at the house unexpectedly, and after a blazing row the shooting took place.

Bell married Augusta in 1982, after serving a six month sentence for a bizarre attack on his first wife Janet. He put her through a humiliating ordeal for allegedly having an affair with another man.

One of Bell's close friends in Coggeshall said that he would be very surprised if he had shot himself, I am not surprised that he lost his temper, but I don't believe he would have turned the gun on himself. He confirmed that he used to meet Bell in local pubs for heavy drinking sessions. He was very popular; he was a man's man and lots of fun.

Norfolk police said they were not looking for anyone else in connection with the shooting. Police confirmed that no one else was in the house at the time of the killings. Post mortem examinations were carried out at Gorleston, near Yarmouth. Millionaire James Bell blasted his pretty young wife to death only four years after their wedding. Public school educated Augusta Walker had been swept off her feet by the man who publicly humiliated his first wife.

Bell was jailed for six months in February 1982 for violence towards his first wife Janet. In a sensational court case, Bell was branded as "cruel" by a judge to punish her for an alleged love affair. Janet Bell left her husband soon after the incident. She had been beaten by Bell, who had threatened to kill himself and someone else close to her "slowly and painfully".

During the trial, Augusta Walker – then only 18 – remained loyal to Bell. At the Bell said Augusta has stuck by me, no one knows how much my wife provoked me, I never want to see her again.

Augusta walker was unperturbed about marrying a man old enough to be her father. Divorce proceedings between Bell and his first wife began.

Augusta insisted that she was not the cause of the split between James and Janet Bell, who had been married for 27 years. Augusta said I have never met Janet. "Jimmy and I met a few months after she left him". And she denied Bell was violent. "I have never seen him in a temper".

Augusta met James Bell at a dinner party; she was impressed by his manners. He sent her flowers and took her out to dinner. It was a lifestyle Augusta was used to. Bell, whose rambling detached home, Bouchier Grange in Coggeshall had been in the family for 50 years – knew how to turn in the charm, but there were rows. Augusta finally walked out on Bell, taking their

18 month old daughter Victoria. It was a decision that led to her death at her parent's home in the tiny Norfolk village of Upper Billingford. No one may ever really know what made Bell snap and take a gun to the mother of his daughter. This was a tragic killing and a mystery to why it happened, remains.

Inquest into Double Shootings – Mr. Bell

The inquest into the violent deaths of famer James Bell and his young wife was opened. Coroner for Diss, Norfolk, Earnest Clark, recorded that the bodies of Mr. Bell, 50, and his 22 year old wife had been identified Mrs Bell's stepfather Michael Goodier of Upper Billingford, Norfolk. Mr. Goodier made the identification after the bodies were discovered by the police.

Mr. Bell had travelled to Norfolk to see his estranged wife, who was staying with her mother. No details of the cause of death were given at the inquest, which was adjourned until September 2nd when it was reopened at Diss Corn Hall. Police had found the bodies of Mr. Bell and his estranged wife Augusta, side by side in her mother's house. Armed police broke into the cottage after a four siege – police found shotgun near the bodies.

I used to visit a bungalow owned by James Bell. It was just across the road from his own luxurious farmhouse. I had reason to go there twice a day for quite a while. During the time I visited it, it was let to man and his English wife. When I first went there they had two children. She had a further child during the time I visited the house as part of my employment.

It came as a great surprise that, after she moved heaven and earth to get her second child enrolled in the local school, because he was still a few months too young to be eligible. However he was actually accepted. As I say, without any knowledge or warning, they moved quickly away one weekend before the second boy started school.

It was a surprise to me as the eldest boy, although coloured, was very popular and a real character, even though he was only about six years of age. He was a colourful dresser and had all the latest American gear. As I stated, this was a very surprising incident. Duty calls, I suppose.

Mr. Bull – Coggeshall

ON Bank Holiday Monday, May 15th, 1985 – millionaire antiques dealer Wilfred Bull shot his wife, Patsy, dead in their showroom – and initially tried to blame her death on intruders. But his attempts to fake a burglary at their plush showroom in West Street, Coggeshall, failed. Eventually he admitted at his Old Bailey trial in March that he shot Patsy – but he claimed it was an accident. A jury decided it was deliberate and he was jailed for life.

Internationally famous Bull, who counted prime ministers among his acquaintances and who mixed with royalty and top people, had rowed with Patsy over his continuing love affair with a brunette from Braintree. Eight year's earlier the couple's Coggeshall Mansion was ravaged in a £150,000 blaze.

Mr. Bull – Coggeshall Antiques

What can be said about Mr. Bull – everyone for miles knew him and his business; he was no stranger to misfortune. Once he accidentally shot and killed his own brother.

Was a quick profit too enticing for him, did he get caught up in an unfulfilled business venture which left him and others at great loss and no profit? Something happened here that is unwritren.

Mr. Bull was famous all over the world, his friends included many top people in both politics and show business and many other distinguished people – a man who had everything – what a tragedy. Money can be a curse!

What does it profit a man if he converts the whole world and all its wealth, and in doing so loses his soul? It is far better to stop worrying about the things you may not have, and enjoy the things that you may have.

Coincidence: Mr. Bamber was farmer and a magistrate. Mr. Bell was a wealthy farmer. Mr. Bull was a prosperous antique dealer. There has certainly been a link between some of these people. There's certainly a grudge bearing on some of the events. It is possible the links are surely chance, or a chain of events and strange circumstances which cannot be explained.

Is there an underworld link? Is this chance or coincidence, or is there a motive linking all of these events which have happened within a few miles vicinity of each other?

These coincidences may be unfortunately somehow linked with the happenings in the Essex area.

Fate travels all roads gathering souls to their destiny. The path which we all have to travel. So pray for guidance for all souls to be given grace to reach life's journey safely.
Be good. It is a short life – enjoy it.

The Rise of Cairns

I write these words because I like Coggeshall. I like very much the times I have spent here working. When I first started work in Coggeshall, Candor Motors had just closed their garage in Coggeshall. The garage was in the centre of the main street set back from the road. A Mr. Cairns was in business from near there, his business deals were varied.

Several people who got caught up in his business lost sums of money, including Colchester solicitor Jimmy Neale; I don't feel the true facts have come out of this case. People have lost because of the associated dealings.

I write this article because of distress people have suffered. Rumours are not always based on truth. There are angry people about.

It must be fully understood by all readers that I do not believe Mr. Cairns' dealings had anything whatsoever to do or are linked with any of the tragedies mentioned in this book.

Coggeshall Man – Tommy

An old local man, Tommy, who used to catch rabbits with his whippet dog, once told me he was just climbing through a hedge with a cock pheasant, when a policeman stopped him. He said, "Look officer, this pheasant has just attacked me". When he was told to empty his pockets, he had six eggs. Tommy quoted an ancient bylaw which meant he could only be fined a shilling (5p) an egg.

He told me once while rabbitting late one night, he saw a coven at Marks Hall. A young maiden was plied with drink and tired to a tree. The coven danced around the naked maiden till she screamed in ecstasy.

He told me several locals have in the past seen similar events. Marks Hall was once a camp for early Romans. Some local gossip says Queen Boadicae is buried with her chariot and jewels in the parish of Coggeshall.

Covens and Witchcraft

People may think that witchcraft is long gone by. Essex is a very progressive and cosmopolitan county. I reckon Essex is the most progressive county in England. Society caters for all of its needs. The activities that take place throughout the county of Essex are unbelievable. So it would be no great surprise to the people to suggest that covens exist in Essex.

The legality or the morals of these goings on, are no concern of mine; leave well alone I was told.

I enclose a selection of information which I collected from rubble taken from a house being renovated in Coggeshall. Some had been translated partly from Latin, so all of the details are what was as near as possible written years ago. They are now in some sort of order.

Strange events happened after a full sized cat and other items were disturbed when builders removed articles from a Coggeshall house during renovation work.

The tales and happenings in Coggeshall recently are like the script of a "Tales of the Unexpected" story.

Coggeshall Barn Wins Top Award

Essex received three commendations in the Civic Trust Awards 1986. The environmental awards scheme attracted a record number of entries – 1,1,23 – including 22 from Essex.

The judges said the repair and reinstatement of the historic barn had been impeccable carried out by the Coggeshall Grange Barn Trust.

Monte Carlo

As I said, I previously won a holiday to Monte Carlo. This was an enlightening trip from flying in an aeroplane to Nice in France and being picked up at the airport and flown in a helicopter to Monaco, the home of Prince Rainer, also the home of the late Grace Kelly. I was not terrifically impresses with Monte Carlo. I feel it is vastly overrated, and is ridiculously expensive, which is an unnecessary expense, like food and drink. On an evening there is often a terrible stench in the air. It is hilly and a very small place, the beach is not as big as a football pitch. The casino is a one-arm Mecca, the museum is spas and uninteresting. The main hotel the De Paris might have been wonderful years ago. Some of the American guests were probably older. There are some nice yachts in the harbour. Monaco is on a hill: I liked Monaco, the best things are free, that is the warmth and the colours. Monaco church is where Grace Kelly is buried.

The church is a grey building with a centre aisle, a left hand walk and a right hand walk. The alter is at the end of the church. There are alcoves with statues and paintings, there is a semi circle behind the alter where the Grimaldis and Princess Grace are laid underneath slabs; her burial slab is on the left of the alter.

After my wife and I left the alter I lit some candles for thanksgiving. I was walking back towards the entrance of the church, when two shafts or rays of light shone down from the roof of the inside of the church. You could see distinctly the brightness; although there were two shafts of light it was only about an inch wide. There was no reason why it should have been there and we could not see where it came from, so I placed my hands under the shafts or beams of light, so it shone on the inside of my hands. My wife did the same, then the lights left, there was a nice smell of perfume when this happened. I felt a tingle in my hands after leaving the church in Monaco, and walking down towards Monte Carlo we stopped at Baden Baden Terraces.

These terraces overlook the sea, it is a lovely view. They were opened by Grace Kelly. I decided to take a photograph of my wife as she sat on a wall; behind her was a large palm tree. As I started to focus the camera, all around us the wind seemed to get stronger and the sea to rise, but close to us it was calm. I remember a blue white light and I took the photograph. I said to my wife that I had a vision; she said it's too much wine. Later, when the film was developed, there was a face which has appeared on the film. Was this chance, luck or coincidence, or was I meant to go? Did Marilyn Monroe send me a message?

The events which have taken place have left me with a spiritual awakening. It is utterly impossible to convey the feeling of greater understanding and knowledge. I am just an instrument being manipulated. Although I feel I am being guided to be a spiritualistic healer, perhaps in times to some I will have a fuller understanding of the subject. I am totally convinced there is a spiritual life after the death of the body.

"It is a glittering high rise village of total expense, where memories of Princess Grace as never to far away."

Imagine you have struck it rich and want to join the Monaco jet set. A swish apartment must be your first purchase. Call on an estate agent where property experts recommend the 13th floor Park Palace block.

At £2,800,000 it is extremely good value, it has four bedrooms – each with bathroom – heated swimming pool, and a terraced garden overlooking Casino Square and the Mediterranean. Next you'll need a yacht – how about something like a 150ft cruiser with 1,960 horsepower engines and a crew of five to maintain? A marine broker says you must add 10% annually for running costs, insurance, fuel and mooring fees.
Now for the car. Not a Rolls Royce – far too common in these parts. A Lamborghinis fits the bill; capable of 185mph. A 1987 model with less than 1,000 miles on the clock. Price: £95,000. But hurry – it's a rare catch,

Monte Carlo

You must of course, dress the part. A silver silk double breasted suit from Valentino's will cost you £835. For your wife, a ball gown with black velvet top and classic lace skirt over silk will cost £3,500. Lastly, jewellery from Cartier. A full set of necklace, earrings, bracelet and ring studded with diamonds and rubies costs £795, 625.

Total price for your new image: nearly £5.4 million. Time for cocktails with the Sinara's……

Champagne corks pop into the Mediterranean. It is cocktail house in Monte Carlo…….paradise on earth.

Step into the Hotel de Paris and you are in a world of wall to wall millionaires, stars and beautiful people.

The names themselves seem to drip with money. Niarchos, Estee Lauder, Sinatra, Roger Moore, Khashoggi…..

Outside, mere mortals gather on the pavement to gaze in awe at the super rich. It is the greatest show on earth.

Tourists arrive by coach load to rub shoulders with money. Cameras click as movie stars and millionaires draw up in their limousines, casually throwing re keys to cream suited doormen directing the world's most exclusive traffic jams.

A white Bentley Mulsanne Turbo – every inch of its chrome gleaming in the 80 degree heat – is squeezed into a space beside a silver-grey Aston Martin Lagonda.

Rolls Royces? There are too many to count. Ferraris too, nearly every one red. A large breasted Italian girl pouts seductively next to a midnight blue Lamboughini. This is her day trip to dreamland. Inside the Hotel de Paris, barman Louis is pouring Roederer Cristal champagne for the who's who of showbiz royalty. Tonight it's Joan Collins, John Forsyth and Charlton Heston – and myself.

The celebrities pass virtually unnoticed – as does a former teacher from Essex, sitting at his usual table. Ignoring Joan Collins at elbow, he sips chilled Chablis and announces, "Everyone is equal here" that's the great thing about it. Equal that is, because millionaires are ten-a-penny in Monte Carlo.

Once a £6,000 a year schoolmaster struck gold with a series of books on teaching English as a Foreign Language. They netted him million and he moved here almost 11 years ago "to join the rich idle". He admits there is no pretence. "I came here to escape the British taxes, purely and simply. Now

it costs me an arm and a leg to get legless in the most expensive bar in the world. Even a glass of water costs £5"A tall American walks in, saying: "hi, see you can still afford to drink" He is well known aging gigolo. He sits in his own chair and at his own table. It is the same for most of the other well heeled customers. Night after night the cast and the dialogue stay the same. "That is how they squeeze the rich in Monte; they pay more for their booze." A woman with enormous sunglass walked in and was asked:"why are you wearing those bloody ridiculous spectacles?"
She pulled them down to her chin and said: "That's why" It was Liza Minelli. Barman Louis juggles his cocktail shaker like a maracas-player in a Latin dance band. Sinatra calls him "The Maestro" and it's reputed he's the highest paid barman in the Riveria. Monte Carlo is simply the most stylist place in the world.

Suddenly it's time for everyone to go home – or back to the Hotel de Paris, where guests are preparing to change for dinner.

In the cocktail bar, waft of Shalimar perfume by Guerlain, drifts in – followed by a pert middle – aged woman with raven hair and alabaster skin, teetering on four inch heels.
She seems to be taking a sizeable portion of jewels on walkabout. On her wrist is a gold bangle two inches wide set with amethysts, pearls, sapphires and a glittering diamond.
Her introduction to the lotus life was sudden. She sold some shares and her accountant told her to get out of England fast, so she said, "I came here to Monte Carlo at the start of the tax year. Now I am enjoying myself. The time to be happy is now." She is staying in the pampered splendour of a £300 a night suite at t Hotel de Paris.
"I adore Monte Carlo", she says in a thick European accent. "It is some glamorous. People look so beautiful." You are never overdressed here. A girl can wear her jewels without feeling someone is going to steal them. I saw Frank Sinatra and his wife the other night surrounded by four bodyguards. Like most of Monaco's elite, they parade from one select establishment to another. The Hotel de Paris, The Sorting Club, Rompoldi's, The Conway Club, Café de Paris and Jimmy-Z-Nightclub. If you can't the rich at one of these places, the chances are they have left town – or are staying at home. A mineral water cost £4 minimum. A magnum of champagne will set you back

£190. It is where the spending habits of the young put their wealthier elders to shame.

Champagne is THE drink in Monte Carlo. The Hotel de Paris, where it costs about £60 a time, serves 2,000 bottle per week.

There is very little crime in Monte Carlo. Old ladies walk about with diamonds as big as strawberries. They pay expensively to be seen in the razzamatazz of fake glory. It is well worth a walk up in winding, hilly staircase to Monaco, where the palace guards look like tin soldiers of bygone days and the huge cannons now a replica of the past. A leisurely walk round the few gift shops and to vie the church is a very pleasant stroll in the sunshine. I met several famous people during my stay at the Hotel de Paris. One was a bodyguard for a famous celebrity. We used to play darts. He tried everything to beat me, but couldn't.

He gave me a pack of playing cards as a present – I nearly collapsed when I saw what the photograph was on the back of them.

I liked my flight in the helicopter from Nice in France to Monaco. The Hotel bedroom had a bar fridge with all types of drinks inside it. It was the size of a small house fridge, yet I was told the drinks, if you were foolish enough to drink them, would cost thousands. I also attended a famous diamond sale with free champagne. Tiaras and rings worth millionaires were on display, including black pearls.

An American lady gave me a £100 bottle of champagne for picking up a glass which she had accidentally knocked over. It costs about £20 just to have someone park our car. The only way I would go back to Monte Carlo is if someone else would pay for me.

Still, I am thankful and very grateful for the privilege and experiences of being able to go there, a chance which is rarely given to ordinary people of this world. I stayed at the Hotel de Paris during my visit. The memory will stay with me forever.

The cards which were given to me are too unsavoury to be seen or published. The subject which they portray may well be the reason why Marilyn Monroe committed suicide. This is my opinion.

A wealthy American lady at Monte Carlo did ask me to go to Texas for a vacation to discuss the issue. But I reluctantly decline the offer for obvious reasons.

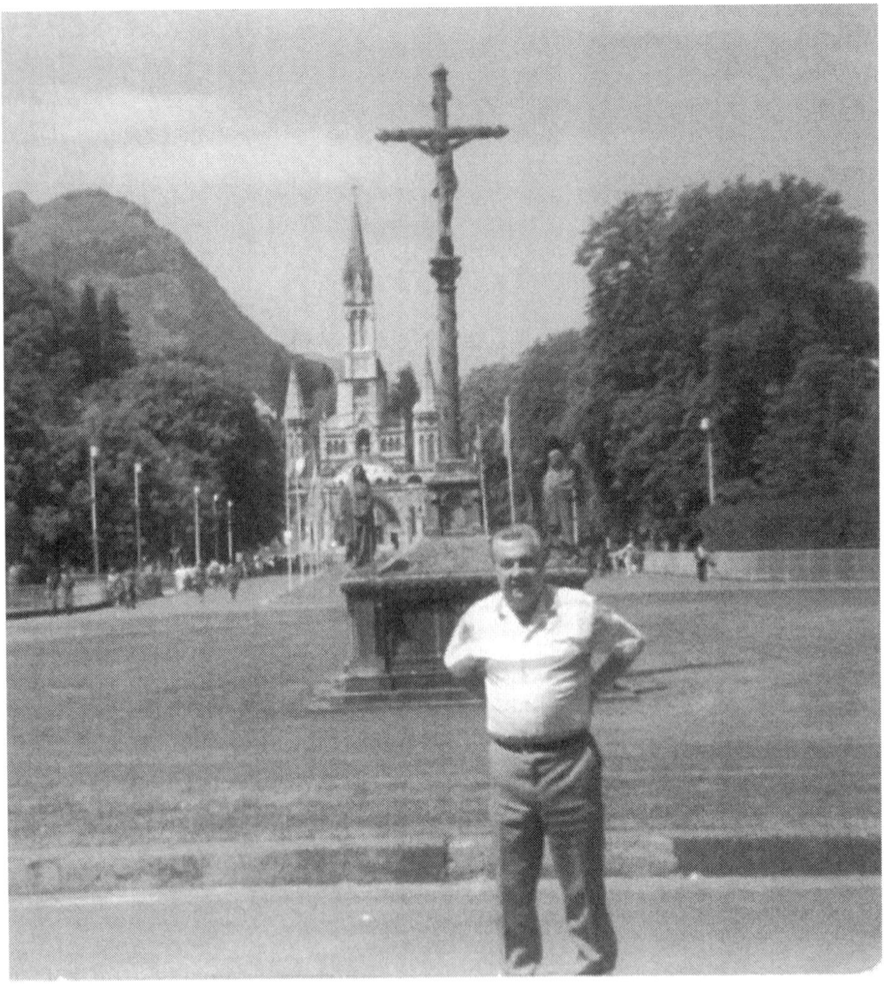

United Faith Healing Foundation

Dear Friend

You are now being Helped by absent Healing.
Every Morning at 7 p.m. and 7 a.m. in the evening.
Please let us know at least once a month the way you feel.
We hope sincerely that through the Power of Prayer and Faith
you may soon be well again.

                God Bless You
                    Kind regards
                          (Chairman) Peter T. Healey

        15 Bull Lane, Tiptree, Essex CO5 0BE

THE KEY TO HEALTH

A great gift of Healing is yours to find,
If you will penetrate your thoughts inside your mind,
Into the hidden secret depths of solitude and rest,
There will you find sanctuary of the Blest.

I know the feelings of the troubled soul,
Who seeks to find peace of mind where troubles flow,
Yet there in the mind, If you care to control,
Is the greatest gift for miricles yet, to Unfold.

Inside the mind are messages divine,
and gifts untold are yours to find,
Mysterious Healing Powers are within Oneself,
But only you yourself can unlock the gift and set yourself free,
Yes only you yourself possess the key,
The Key to unlock your mind.

                              Peter T. Healey

Healing

After the holiday to Monte Carlo, I settled down to normal living again. Delusions of grandeur are OK if you can afford them. However, I could not get this face of a vision out of my mind. A musical box in the house where we lived started to play by itself, which is mechanically impossible. However, it did the toe cap fell off one of my work boots during the night, and a few other strange things happened.

Well, I came to the decision that I would seek professional advice, so I went to see my parish priest. He was understanding and helpful. Canon Dobson was his name. He visited the house, sprinkled Holy water around and said prayers. He also presented me with a crucifix to keep. Everything seemed settled in the house. But in myself I felt uneasy and unsettled. One day I was talking to a woman who couldn't move her wrist. I said I could heal her hand. I held her hand for half a minute. I felt a tingling sensation. The woman went home. I saw her three days later, her hand and wrist were cured.

Another lady came to me who had been a hairdresser for many years,. She was severely troubled with her hands. I did healing with my hands and a prayer. I saw her a week later; she said it was a miracle. She had visited all the specialists for treatment. Weeks later in a car park, this same lady brought another lady and asked me to make healing on her hands, as she severed quite severely. This was 2pm. I did a healing, by 4om, this lady's hands were better.

Another lady had been in an awful car smash, she would not leave home; she lost weight and was distressed. I did a healing on this lady; she is now active and gets about. I have been told she has just been to France for a holiday.

However, I did not really want to be a healer. I felt terribly embarrassed. I never charged payment for my healing. But after healing I seemed to transfer the symptoms from the person to myself, which can be unpleasant.

I felt unsettled and felt a strange spirit or force around me, so I decided to go back to my parish priest. I asked for exorcism. I am a Catholic, but my parish priest was very reluctant to give me exorcism, so I was left with this strange uneasiness.

I mentioned this to the vicar of Coggeshall, where I worked. He invited me to discuss my problem with him.

I'm the meantime, I visited Walsingham to see the shrine. However, I felt no better. I went back to see the Reverend David at Coggeshall. I asked for exorcism. He told me he would have to have a word with the parish priest. However, after a great deal of effort and persuasion, he did decide to give me a blessing. I went after being given permission from the Bishop to perform the exorcism. I was blessed, and during the blessing a ranting and raving spirit left me. It left me very weak and tired. During my blessing I had a psychic message telling me I was going to win a small amount of money, then a larger amount of money.

When I won the second amount of money, I was told to get a carving Madonna for the church – part thanksgiving, part penance. I said to the vicar: now remember what my message was, that I am going to win some money, then I have to buy a Madonna. He said: I will remember. The following week I won a small amount on the football pools, I though how strange, and then I thought I would visit the parish church at Coggeshall, for thanksgiving for my exorcism. Father David was having a healing ceremony, I attended the healing service. Shortly afterward, I won £2,000. I went immediately back to see the Revered David. I said to him: what did I say to you after exorcism? He said: you told me you would win a small amount of money, and then a large amount of money and you would buy a Madonna. I said, well that has happened, and I am frightened if I don't buy the Madonna something may happen, so he said go ahead and buy the Madonna, which I did. It is carved from one piece of wood and I five feet tall. Was this chance, luck or coincidence?

Storms – The worth in Living Memory

!987 – October 15th/16th
Part of my book is about strange happenings; some events can be explained, some are just mere coincidence others casual. The last event before going to press is the storm which occurred during the night of October 15th / 16th, 1987.

Awakened by the sound of our bedroom door being opened by a sudden burst of wind. I got out of bed to close a small window in the bedroom. The noise of the wind was terrific, the sky was full of flashes and glows of red light were filling the bedroom with flashes of light; there was no thunder. As I drew the curtains to close the window, I looked out; a strange sight appeared below me: it was probably a trick of the light, an illusion, or a bit of everything. My mind was convinced it saw the Devil as he went through the sky, he hit a big elder tree in the next garden, uprooting it and smashing a fence panel to pieces. Strange, coincidence, illusion or true – I don't know.

The flood from the heavy rain was unbelievable – it was possible to paddle a canoe up the main road in Coggeshall, Essex. The spirit that guides the weather was very angry. Some people believe it was a warning of things yet to come, possible a large earthquake – who know?

The "Old" New Times, Tiptree

One of my first pints of beer was in the "old" New Times in Tiptree. It was owned by the Gray family brewers; later on Ridley's Brewery supplied some beers there. I myself liked the Grays beer. It was a very small pub, but I thoroughly enjoyed many a good time there. Two sisters ran the place. One sister was Amy (her daughter was a very famous opera singer); Maud was the other sister. I believe she was the licensee. She is one of life's characters: and was driving her car even though she is over 80 years of age. Both sisters were very strong Freemasons: both have been Grand Lady of their Lodge.

Another character helped these two sisters and used to look after the pub. Originally he was from Cornwall; Bert was his name, but he was known as the Major, he was a dapper man and had a military look about him. He sported a small moustache, with silver pushed back hair.

He was a terrific storyteller. It was an education to sit and listen to him, especially when he went off beer and on to Scotch whisky. I was asked to join the Freemasons. I was seconded and proposed, but when I filled in my application form, it asked for my religion. I put Roman Catholic. At this time the lodge concerned refused Catholics because they go to confession. Although I did not join the Freemasons, I did get invited to a Ladies' Night as a guest as the George Hotel, Colchester – I was guest of Maude, licensee of the "old" New times; my wife was also involved.

I was to pick up Maude and her sister Amy at the "New Times". When I arrived, Bert, the Major, said to me: "where are you going?" I had a black evening suit on, dickie bow tie. I wore a pair of brown suede boots. Bert told me I couldn't go to a Freemasons evening wearing suede boots, I had to wear dress shoes.

I said I didn't possess a pair of dress shoes. Bert said I could borrow his – they fitted me around the instep and the heel, but the toe part was too long. They were made of shinny patent leather.

We all finished up at this dinner dance. A friend of Maude's, a widow, kept asking me to dance with her; several times she stood on my toes. We all had a very good time. Later the next day when I went to return the shoes, I noticed a dent where my toes should have been. I went to see Bert and explained the marks on his shoes. I told him I would buy him another pair. I asked him how much they were and he said 328 but would settle for £25 – which I accepted.

Well, when the Major got any money, he liked to walk to the Ship Inn for a pint or two. Once when he returned to the New Times he got drunk. Maude asked me to carry him across the road and put him to bed. I took off his tie, coat and shoes and laid him on the bed to sleep it off.

It was a few days before I went back to the old New Times. I mostly went in there weekends, except in the summer when I called there more often. When I next went to the pub, Bert was not there. I asked Maud where he was. She said Bert was sulking because he had lost his false teeth, some of which were gold capped.

Well, after a week of no Bert in the pub, life was the same. Anyway, Amy sent him to a private dentist to be fitted with new false teeth, including gold caps as before. When he got his teeth. Bert was his old self again. He told Amy they cost £150 – they cost £140 – so Bert kept £10 for a drink. He had a good session on the beer, on the way home he sprained his ankle. After a few day's rest, he could not get his shoes on, so Maude said, "cut the dress shoes" which he had lent me. He said that was a good idea. When he went to put his foot in the dress shoe, he found his teeth which he had lost!
The old New Times is now closed and there is now a "new" New Times. The old new Times had some good customers. Lord Hillingdon, who owned Messing Park, Wing Commander Jim Barlow, Nobby. Mr. Munro, Jim and his pal John, the village blacksmith with his friends EV and his wife, old Paddy the Irishman – a very friendly crowd.

The "old" New Times (above) with its newly-built namesake (below).

Bert, the Major

Ole Bert the Major used to drink in the New Times in Tiptree. One day he worked behind the bar whilst Manny was out. Manny's dog bit Bert. When Manny told me about this, I said, "How is Bert?" He said: Bert is alright but the dog's got alcohol poisoning.

Bert the Major has now passed away. But with his patter I am sure he will be able to visit the Times and rattle the glasses.
Squadron-Leader Jimmy "The Wag" Williamson said:

It was hard doing it,
But when I did it
It was well worth it.

Another of the characters.

The "Ship", Tiptree

I have mixed feeling about The Ship. When I first visited the The Ship, the landlord was retired Welseguardsman, Ev, and his wife. They were a very well-liked couple. When they retired, his daughter Mary and her husband took over the pub. Mary and Jim split up and both remarried.

When Jim got married again, his new wife stayed at The Ship. Not long after being married, Jim was tragically killed in a car accident.

Another blow struck. One of Jim's friends, who was visiting, collapsed and died. This is sad but true. Jim came from Jarrow in the North of England. I got on very well with him.

As I've stated, I've got mixed feelings about The Ship, although it is my favourite pub, so I wish well to anyone who has any sort of association with it. It is lovely olde worlde type of place, the food is excellent, probably the best pint of Trueman's Special Bitter for miles.

There is an air of mystery surrounding The Ship. I don't think this will be the last time I will write about The Ship. Give it a visit, it is well worth it. It has won several prizes for a good hospitality. It has a mature atmosphere and is extremely popular for a good meal and welcome. The friendly landlady will always make anyone welcome.

All the best people visit The Ship.

Two views of "The Ship" public house, Tiptree.

The "Ship", Tiptree

Pigeon Club

As I said, I kept racing pigeon. I belonged to the Tiptree and District Club. It was a new club with headquarters at a pub called the Prince of Wales at Inworth, just outside Tiptree.

The previous club was at Witham. I enjoyed most of the time when the club was in Inworth, we had a very good secretary, Mr. Taffy Eaves.

The pub landlord left to buy his own pub, so the pigeon club moved to new premises at the Tiptree United Football Club. After moving there, the pigeon club got bigger, and the atmosphere changed. It became less and less friendly.

The pigeon club was in trouble with the Royal Pigeon Association. The club was put on supervision for six months. I finished up resigning from the pigeon club, as I was disgusted with certain member's attitudes.

I am no longer associated in any way with racing pigeons – pigeon racing can be a pain in a the arse. But good luck to anyone for trying!

You not have to be daft to keep pigeons, but it helps if you are!

The last four or five years in England, Ireland, Scotland and Wales a disease of epidemic proportions has hit racing pigeons. Thousands of birds have been destroyed. Racing in some areas has been banned. Inoculation of pigeons has been compulsory to race in some organizations. The disease is a killer: it has similar symptoms on pigeons as AIDS has on humans. Strange coincidence – but true.

I had 12 racing pigeons from the Queen's private lofts at Sandringham and Len Rush's loft at King's Lynn, Norfolk.

Len Rush was the Queen's Royal Loft manager for many years. I bought sold, and exchanges pigeons with the Queen's manager. My Pigeons had the Queen's personal ER ring on their legs. They originated from gift birds from the King of Belgium to the Queen Mother. They were Dellmotte Jurions and Janson strain.

Strange Encounter

My job took me in and around, if not all of, Coggeshall and a great area of Essex. The views and the places I have visited will remain with me forever.

Part of my job was to pick up children living in areas too far to walk to school. Many interesting things have occurred whilst doing this job. I remember one evening going to pick up some children. When we entered the mini bus, there was a small boy. I said "what are you doing here?" He said "You have to take me home". I said "what do they call you?" He said, "James Bond"

I made enquiries about the boy. What had happened was his parents had brought him to school on his first morning, but no one had informed me. After this I called him 007½. I took the boy to and from school for several years.

One day going to pick him up I noticed a For Sale notice. His parents has intended selling their property. It was in a very remote place. It was on the market for some time. One day I said to the boy's mother, if you changed the front door and landscape the approach, the house would sell. The mother asked me if I knew anyone who did landscape gardening. I said I didn't, but if I met anyone I would let her know.

Well, the old New Tines closed; another new pub was built next door to the original New Times. The new landlord and his wife and family same from Southend, Essex; they had been running the famous Minerva r=there. They were a fantastic couple; they brought modern times to Tiptree.

Manny Devito was the landlord's name, with his lovely wife Sylvis. I used to go to the New Times on a weekend the same as the old New Times. One weekend I mentioned the landscape gardening to Manny. He told me to see a lady customer at the pub. He said a friend of hers was a landscape gardener.

I did as Manny suggested and had a word with her. She said she would send her friend Richard round to see me on Sunday morning. This chap came round to our house. My wife made a cup of tea. The chap had a beard and fairly long hair, but his eyes were dead and lifeless. He was a weird person to meet. He sat down in our house and rolled his own cigarettes. He asked me what I wanted done in the garden. I explained to him that the garden work was not for me but for a person in Coggeshall. I said I would phone the lady and see if she still needed the work to be done.

She said she did still require the work, but would like a drawing and an estimate. This chap Richard asked me if I would take him to the address as he had no car. I did take him to see the lady, and he was given the job.

A week later he asked me to lend him some money for equipment to carry out the job. He did the job; everyone was pleased with his work. I never did get my money back.

My wife said to me "Pete, do me a favour, don't ever bring him to this house again. She said to me he has an evil look about him.

Richard was paid well for this job. I did ask several times about my money, but it was useless asking as he appeared to be living it up with his friends.

After this I stopped going to the New Times. However, one day a friend of mine stopped me early one morning and said there had been a murder in Tiptree, up the West End Road. A few days later I read in the paper how a man had been caught in Wakefield, Yorkshire, after stealing a car from Tiptree. It turned out to be Richard r=the gardener. He had murdered the lady in Tiptree. What was stranger, he had just finished a term of Imprisonment – he was sentenced to life.

Some weeks later I met the lady who had her garden landscaped. She was on the car park at Coggeshall with a flat tyre. I changed the wheel for her, and told her about the gardener, she nearly collapsed.

She told me she had had a new door put on her house and the garden landscaped, had re-advertised the house and sold it for more than previously advertised, and has now moved away from Coggeshall.

Since writing these stories, Manny and Sylvia Devito have passed away. Words fail to express my sorrow. I can only say Rest in Peace and blessings to your family. It was a pleasure to meet you both.

Football Match

I don't know why, but one Saturday I decided to go to the local football ground and see Tiptree –United play Braintree. They are generally hard-fought games and I have friends and family who live in Braintree. Towards the end of the game, two players collided in the goal area whilst going for a high ball; one Braintree player was knocked unconscious and I went over to see if he was alright.

I was a spectator and I massaged his heart which had stopped. Michael Hunt from Tiptree moved his arms and breathed into him. After what seemed to be ages, he woke up and said: "I've been to heaven". I honestly thought the man had died. He took some time to come round. I thought something had guided me to Tiptree football ground that day.

Coincidence, chance or luck……………………..

Feering

For many years I had to attend the small school at Feering to deliver mail. One day I had not been long out of the school yard when lightning struck the top of the bell tower on the school roof. No one was hurt.

Normally lots of children play in the small playground. The falling bricks could have proved very harmful if anyone had been in the playground: someone kept us safe that day.

Another day, travelling from Tiptree through Inworth to Kelvedon one wintry morning, a furniture van skidded on black ice and knocked over a power carrying telegraph pole. The weather was awful at the time.

The furniture van turned over on its side, the broken pole lay across the van door; the other door was on the road, sparks were flying everywhere, diesel oil was pouring into the road, the engine of the van was still running. I thought there might be a fire. The driver and passenger were trapped. I picked up a shovel, moved the sparking wires to one side. I smashed the van window and helped to get the two men free from the van and I stopped the engine running.

Another motorist phones the police, ambulance and fire brigade. The road was blocked for a long time.

I was late getting to Coggeshall that morning – those two men were lucky. I am sure that if I had not broken the windscreen and turned off the van's engine, it would most certainly have caught fire.

How to Develop Magical Powers

In order to acquire magical powers it is first necessary to discipline your mind. The average person has no real control over his mind. Thoughts come and go will-nilly and he finds it very difficult to concentrate for long periods. Yet to achieve one's desires in magic it is essential that one can project a beam of Mind Energy carrying the Thought Image of the thing desired.

Once you learnt to do this successfully you can contact the highest reaches of the mind that in turn activate The Universal Creative Mind, The Life Force, that can create circumstances to bring you your desire. The aim of this lesson is to teach you to discipline your mind. Once you have mastered it you will find your powers of concentration will be considerably improved. Be sure to master this task before you attempt the next one, otherwise you will make little progress.

Useful Methods
Go to a quiet room where you will not be disturbed for half an hour and sit in a comfortable chair. Allow yourself to relax and close your eyes; place your hands in such a position that they will not disturb you by weighing upon your stomach. Permit your mind to wander where it will, making no attempt to direct your thoughts or control them in any way. In this task you need to detach your mind from your brain, like disengaging the clutch on a car and permitting it to freewheel.

You will find that all sorts of things will go through your mind. You will drift away to pleasant spots and observe the events taking place there. It will be like looking into a clairvoyant's crystal and all manner of things will be revealed to you. All the time you must passively follow the pictures in your mind and just drift along with them.

You will find this most relaxing, you will be in a sort of wakeful sleep in which the subconscious mind will be able to come to the surface and so gradually, in later tasks, be able to accept commands for the conscious mind and so enable you to visualise the things you need and project a magical energy beam carrying the image of you desire.

You should perform this task for half an hour, if possible, at the same time in the same room as each day for two weeks. When you can do this and feel completely relaxed after it you will be ready for the next task.

Method 2
Now that you can successfully meditate upon definite train of thoughts you are ready to move on to a more advanced exercise. Go to your quiet room and allow yourself to completely relax. This time I want you to hold in your mind a single idea, a single thought or picture. You must not permit any other thought to intrude while you hold the original idea in your mind. For example, take the word moon or form in your mind's eye a picture of the moon. Hold this thought or picture in your mind's eye, to exclusion of all else. You will find this quite difficult at first. You may find you can hold your thought or picture for only a minute at first try, but persevere until you can hold the thought or picture in your mind for ten minutes at a time.

This task is the most important one to master because to achieve your objectives in a magical endeavour it is essential that you are able to see clearly in your mind's eye the thing you desire. The next best thing is to have a clear idea in your mind. An idea takes complete possession of your mind so that it becomes an impulsive, passionate desire that cannot be denied. Once you are able to do this and have mastered the tasks that follow, you will be able to project a beam of psychic energy of desire to activate forces that create the circumstances to make your desire a fact.

Method 3
To direct you beam of psychic energy you need to spend a period of absolute quite, relaxed, with your mind a complete blank. Go to your bedroom

at a time when you will not be disturbed for half an hour. Lie upon your bed, close your eyes and relax completely. Empty your mind of all thoughts and ideas. Rigorously exclude any stray thought that may try to enter your consciousness. Make your mind a complete blank.

Many people find this task quite impossible when they first attempt it, yet it is essential that you master this particular task before attempting the next for it is only be relaxing your mind you exclude all matter from it and so prepare for the important desire Picture Thought you will project on your beam o=f psychic energy to make magic work for you.

The more proficient you become in blanking out all the unnecessary thought from your mind before exercising your magical powers, the more successful you will be. Persevere with this task until you can achieve 10 minutes of mind blankness but be careful you do not fall into hypnotic sleep.

Useful Methods of Visualisation
The next step in your studies is to practise to develop you ability to visualise in your mind's eye the things you desire or the circumstances you wish to bring about. You begin by concentrating your attentions upon the ordinary everyday things you do. For example: when you get out of bed in the morning and dress, pay attention to what you are doing. Don't dress automatically without thinking but pay attention. Let your mind observe your actions. Tie your shoes with a deliberate thinking action, and if you use make up, pay more attention than usual to what you are doing.

At breakfast, don't eat automatically while reading the newspaper. Put aside the paper and let your mind dwell upon the action of eating. This may seem a vey simple exercise. But in fact it is nothing of you will soon increase rapidly your powers of concentration that are essential in the practice of ritual magic.

In the next lesson you will be taught a magical ritual for money. To succeed it is essential that you see in your mind's eye, or have a clear idea of exactly your requirement. You should, by closing your eyes during The Ritual, see a clear picture of the precise object you require. If you find this difficult, you must at least have a clear idea of what you want and a passionate desire for it to succeed.

For example: You need £3,500 to buy a car. The first step is to become familiar with the car. Go along to a showroom where the car is on show. Look at it well; become familiar with its shape and detail that by simply closing your eyes at any time a clear picture of the car flashes into your mind. The next step, if possible, is to actually sit in the car. Feel you can own it already. See yourself driving it along your favourite road. See yourself paying for it by cheque. See yourself writing out the cheque and giving it to the salesman.

Once you can do this the next step is to set up your altar and visualise as described and at the same time performing The Ritual for Money or For Any Definite Thing.

The above visualization technique applies to anything you desire. If you need money for a definite purpose visualise yourself receiving it. It is best to start by asking for such a sum as you can see yourself receiving. Do not ask for so large a sum that you have doubts about receiving it. In all magical rites you must be absolutely certain that you will get what you ask for and 99 per cent of people who never succeed in their magical endeavours do not in their hearts believe they will get what they ask for.

So begin by asking for a small sum of money or by asking for some small thing you need or for circumstances to come about for you to achieve some purpose you have your heart set on. It cannot be stressed too much that in the beginning, when using magical ritual believe you will get what you ask for. See it in your mind's eye, or passionately desire it. And don't try to run before you can walk.

Remember. The greater your powers of visualisation, the greater your success in magic. So, from now on, practice bringing to your mind's eye pictures of all manner of simple things to develop your ability.

Ancient Methods of Developing Magic Powers
In all these tasks it is necessary to remain undisturbed in your room for as long as is necessary, therefore be certain that this will be so.

Relax in your comfortable chair as in the previous task, but this time you must select one particular train of thought to dwell upon, allowing no other thought to intrude.

You may choose the seahorse. Think about the sand upon the shore. How came it there? What is its composition, what might be its age? Think about the waves washing upon the beach. Contemplate the ocean, think of the sea in general. What it means to the survival of the human race.

Examine in your mind every aspect of the sea. Or ships and of the men who go to sea in ships. Think of the different types of ships that exist. Take each type of ship you can think of and try and form a picture of it in your mind.

Of course, you don't have to use the sea as you subject for meditation. It can be anything that interests you. But the one essential point about this task is that whatever subject you decide to meditate and contemplate, then this subject, and no other, must be your theme. Any other thought entering you mind must be firmly pushed away.

Each evening, or whatever time you chose for your task, should be more or less the same. And each evening, you must choose a different subject upon which to meditate and contemplate. Whilst doing so, you must try to form mind pictures of your subject. See the ship. See the old tramp steamer and the crew manning the ship. The clearer the picture you form in your mind the greater will be your success in your magical endeavours in later lessons. This task should take about two weeks. When you are satisfied with your progress, learn task three.

Advice and Methods of Candle Burning Spells
There are various methods available to occultists to influence magical forces to act for them. One of the oldest known to man is fire and the simplest way to use fire in ritual magic is by burning candles. The methods used and the equipment and candles used are the subject of this part.

Most of the equipment you will need will be obtainable from The Sorcerers Apprentice, 4-8 Burley Lodge Road, Leeds, West Yorkshire, LS6 1QP. Send them a stamped self-addressed envelope (9in by 4in will do) and ask them for their herbs and oils list and their equipment list.

You need a quite room where you can practice your spells undisturbed, you will need a small altar, any small table or chest will do. You will need two altar cloths, one black, one white. A black robe, a black belt with a ram's head buckle. An old gold coin or any gold item. A silver coin or any silver item. A brass bangle, a quietus skull pendant, a brass chalice, a single disc, swing chain censer foe charcoal, a brass bell, an athame or dagger, parchment, eight small candlesticks, oils for anointing candles, herbs and incense, and a small brush for anointing the candles.

Once you have set up your altar, you will need to furnish it with certain candles, but you need only buy those that are necessary for each individual need you request. The first ritual will be for money to purchase a definite object. You will need two white altar candles, two zodiac candles, one gold candle, six small candlesticks, a gold coin, or gold coin, or gold item, a silver coin, or silver item; an athame or black handled dagger, quietus skull pendant, brass chalice, brass bell, incense burner, disc of charcoal, musk compound oil and matches.

Zodiac or Astral Candles
Aquarius: January 20 – February 18. Blue, green, pink. Pisces: February 19 – March 20. Black, green, yellow. Aries: March 21 – April 19. Pink, rose, white. Taurus: April 20 – May 20. Lemon, red, yellow. Gemini: May 21 – June 21. Light blue, red, and silver. Cancer: June 22 – July 23. Brown, green. Leo: July 24 – August 23. Green, red. Virgo: August 24 – September 21. Black, blue, red. Libra: September 22 – October 21. Black, blue, gold. Scorpio: October 22 – November 21. Black, brown. Sagittarius: November 22 – December 20. Gold, green, red. Capricorn: December 21 – January 19. Black, emerald, pink, white.

Magical Ritual for Money for a Definite Purpose
The following magical candle burning ritual for money to purchase some you need is application to all rituals using candles for money for a definite

purpose. The prayer "Lord of the World" is for guidance only. It is more effective for you to compose your own sincere prayer, but use it until you can make up your own.

Put on your robe and black belt. The psychological effect of proper dress greatly increases your ability to activate the psychic forces. Meanwhile, were any dark attire and your brass bangle.

Lay your altar with a white cloth. At the read of each corner set the white candles in the candlesticks as in the diagram below. In front of there white candle set your zodiac candles slightly inward. Your zodiac candles are those given in the char of your birthdate. In front of the zodiac candle set you golden candle on your right and your silver candle on your left. In the centre of your altar in front set you chalice. To the right of it place your bell. To the left of it your athame or dagger. Place your silver coin or silver item next to you silver candle and your golden coin or golden item next to your golden candle.

Place your incense burner (the swing chain censer on the floor in front of your altar. Put in it a disc of charcoal or whatever charcoal you are able to buy. Have a box of matches handy. Your altar should look like this:

White Candle		White Candle
Zodiac Candle		Zodiac Candle
Silver		
Gold		
Coin		
Coin		
Dagger	Chalice	Bell

Before starting your ritual, anoint each candle with sandalwood oil. Start at the middle of each candle and using your small brush, paint your candle sparingly from the middle up to the wick then from the middle to the base.

Light each candle on your altar, out a match to your charcoal in your burner and sprinkle a small amount of musk compound oil on the burning charcoal, be sure it is well alight before you sprinkle your oil. Write on a small piece of parchment the amount of money you desire and place the parchment under your old candle.

Pour a small amount of whisky in to the chalice; roll it around your mouth before swallowing. Swing your incense burner from side to side, and say in a low clear voice whilst visualizing in your mind's eye the article your desire.

"Lord of the World. Source of all riches. Master of Wealth and Plenty grant to your servant, (your name here) what which I desire. I need 9say how much you need) to purchase (state article required) I send up purifying flame in your name and beseech that you grant my wish.

Repeat this ritual each day until your wish is granted.

Your candle should burn for at least an hour after each ritual.

Advice on Magical Healing Candles Rites
All that is necessary in magical healing is to burn six white candles whilst visualizing the necessary treatment. Lay your altar with a white altar cloth and place six candles that have anointed with oil of eucalyptus, three at the rear of the altar and three at the front. Light the candles and allow them to burn for one hour.

To heal yourself of any complaint you must still your conscious mind and put yourself in the care of your subconscious mind. Go to your quiet room and sit in your comfortable chair and close your eyes. Put your hands upon your knees and permit your mind to wander for a while. When you feel at ease and relaxed imagine that you are surrounded by a pale blue light. Feel this smoothing light penetrating to every part of your body.

Now look mentally at your complaint. For example, a simple headache may be cured by visualizing kindly hands massaging the point of pain and other soothing hands massaging the tendons in your neck.
Say: "Hands of Mercy, Hands of Power, cure my pain and hurt this hour. Let the healing power flow upon my body and bestow blessings of health and ease."

More serious afflictions can be relieved by the following method. Imagine you are surrounded by the Blue Light of health, you wish to treat a knee that you believe is arthritic. See in your mind's eye the bones of your knee. In your imagination gently bathe in green healing oil to sooth away the pain and as pain subsides bathe the knee with white energy rays of healing. You do this by imaging a shaft of warm light is shinning upon your knee.

In magical healing it is essential to possess an excellent picture in your mind of any part of your body you wish to treat. If you do not know what the various parts and organs of the body look like you must get medical book containing sketches, drawings and photographs of them. You will then be able to study the book and know exactly what the part you are treating looks like.

Older men often suffer from an enlarged prostate. The symptom of this complain is the inability to go a full night without getting out of bed several times to pass water. Also people suffering from enlarged prostate find it difficult to pass water generally. To treat this complaint, carry out the preliminary blue light treatment in a completely relaxed state. Then bathe the prostate mentally with green healing oil, seeing soften in your mind's eye. At the same time see that the tube leading to the penis is being relieved by the pressure cause by the enlarged prostate. Since this complete has taken some years to develop you will need to carry out the treatment every day until complete relief is obtained.

The above method of treatment applies to any complaint in your body. See in your mind's eye the organ to be treated. Surround your body mentally with pale blue healing light then treat the affected part with green healing oil. Finish the treatment by bathing the treated part with white healing light.

Personal Healing
Once you have a fair success in healing yourself you are ready to us magical ritual to heal another person. It is not necessary to know the nature of the patient's complaint because the magical healing rays of the Cosmos will seek to sure any illness that is present in the person you seek to heal.

Set up the altar an hour before your patient is due to arrive. Light your four candles and say: "Lord of The Healing Light, heal and banish all pain from (her mention the Patient's name" Repeat this prayer five times. Allow the candles to burn for one hour.

When your patient arrives ask him to sit in the chair provided. Tell him to close his eyes and rest his hands upon his knees. Tell him to imagine that he is entirely surrounded by pale blue light. Now stand behind his chair and place your hands upon his shoulders. Close your eyes and imagine that a pale blue light is flowing from your hands into the shoulders of the patient. Say quietly under your breath, "Lord of Light let this suffering patient (name) be healed this day". Remain with your hands upon the patient's shoulders for about five minutes. Repeat at weekly intervals as necessary.

Distant Healing
Set your altar as described. But this time you pace a white card with your patient's name written upon it in red ink. Once you have your four candles burning say: "Lord of The Healing Light let your healing rays reach out to (name the patient) and make him well and free form pain." All the time you are saying this prayer, imagine the pale blue healing light bathing your patient. You don't need to know what your patient looks like. All that is necessary is to have in your mind's eye a figure, male or female as the case may be, surrounded by the pale blue healing light.

Repeat as often as necessary. If possible tell your patient that healing will take place at a certain time. Ask him to sit quietly in a chair in some place where he will not be disturbed for a quarter of an hour

He must close his eyes and resting his hands upon his knees and imagine that he is surrounded by a pale blue light.

Candle Burning Spell for Good Health
Set up your altar using your white altar cloth. In place of your gold and silver candles you will need white candles. Remove your gold and silver coins or items and replace them with a vessel containing salt and water. Rainwater is best if available. The vessel containing the salt and water should be up front

in the middle of the altar. You need about one tablespoon of salt to about half a pint of water.

Anoint your candles with oil of eucalyptus. You will have on you altar two white candles and two zodiac candles. Put a fresh disc or charcoal in your incense burner, light it and sprinkle upon it oil of eucalyptus for good health. Stand in front of your altar attired in your black robes but not wearing your black belt. With your eyes closed say: "Lord of Harmony, Giver of Wealth and Peace, bathe me in your healing rays and make me well." As you are saying this swing your incense burner too and fro.

While you are saying this you must see yourself in good health in your mind's eye and expect to feel the healing power at work within you. Perform this ritual each Sunday evening until you are well.

If you wish to send forth healing rays to benefit another person, in place of the word "me", utter instead the name of the person you wish to benefit from the ritual.

If possible when sending out healing rays for another person's benefit use some small item of that person's clothing or a piece of hair or a photograph. Allow your candles to burn for one hour after you have concluded the ritual.

General Purpose Rite or Spell
This rite may be used for any purpose for which no specific rite or spell is known. You need two white altar candles, two black candles, and your zodiac candle (plus another person's if used for some matter involving another person. If the birthdate of the person is not known, use a yellow candle. If for a specific sum of money use also a green candle.

You will need your incense burner and charcoal, oil of frangipani, herb of acacia resin, your robe and belt, your quietus skull pendant, your bell and chalice, your athame and a black altar cloth.

Your altar candles go to the rear of the altar left and left. Your athame between the, with the blade pointing away from you. The bell immediately in front of the athame.

Place your zodiac candle to the left of the bell, and if for money, a green candle to the right of the bell. If involving another person whose birthdate is not know, use a yellow candle in place of the green. If the birthdate is known use the appropriate zodiac candle. Place your black candles in front of the altar on the left and right. Fill you chalice with red wine, about a quarter of a pint, or salt and fresh water, place it between the black candles.

Anoint all the candles with oil frangipani and after lighting your incense burner, swing it to and fro saying in a low voice: "Mighty Lord of the Common, hear my prayer, grant my wish I pry, and give my desire" (name your wish here). Kneel in front of the altar after lowering your incense burner to the floor. Repeat the prayers. Rise and allow all candles to burn for one hour. Repeat as often as necessary until your wish is granted.

Oils and Herbs used in Magical Rites and Spells
Oils: Aniseed, sandalwood, cedar wood and lemon grass oil for good luck. Wintergreen oil for money or special requests. Also oil of frangipani. Pine oil for finding a job, promotion or success at work. AmD or civit tint, musk and lime oil for love and faithfulness, lavender oil for harmony, calamus for love and spiritual help or to impose your will upon another person. Eucalyptus for good health and recovery from illness. Lotus oil and mineral oil for magical powers. Magnolia for meditation, oil of patchouli for sexuality. Frangipani oil to be used for any purpose.

Herbs: Star aniseed, good luck and gambling. Asafetida for special requests. Aloes for love, harmony and faithfulness. Eyebright for meditation. Kava-kava root, spiritual help to acquire magical powers. Balm Basil for sexual strength and power over the opposite se. valerian root, success in any activity, work or hobbies.

Procedure: anoint all candles with suitable oil and burn appropriate herbs in your incense burner. Swing it from side to side until the fragrance permeates the room. In the old religions it was thought that the ascending smoke from the burning incense carried up your prayers and pleas to the gods.

Spell for Love and Romance
For this spell you will need your black altar cloth. In place of your gold and silver candles you will need two white altar candles, your zodiac candle and the candle of the person you desire, you need an article of clothing once worn by that person, or a lock of hair or a photograph. You will also need a lock of your own hair. The clothing must not have been laundered since last used by the person desired. You need oils of aloes and herbs of calamus. Anoint your candles with the oil of aloes.

Set your two altar candles in the usual position at the rear of the altar. Place your black candles in front of the altar candles. One slightly to the left, the other slightly to the right. Set your own zodiac candle and the zodiac candle of the desired one in front of and slightly to the left and right of the black candles. Place the lock of hair in front of your zodiac candle and the item of clothing or what you managed to get of the desired one in front of the other zodiac candle. Place your athame to the right of the altar and your bell to the left in front of the clothing.

Put a fresh disc of charcoal in your incense burner and light it. Sprinkle upon it herbs of calamus. Swing your burner from side to side filling the air with the aroma of calamus. Then place your burner upon the floor in front of your altar. Mover your zodiac candle and your lock of hair towards the clothing and the other zodiac candle. Ring the bell, step back and say quietly: "Lord of Love and Desire, bring my love nearer to my side" (in your mind's eye see your desired person in your arms) Return to the altar, take up your incense burner and swing it once more. Return to the spot in front of the altar. Go up to the altar and move the hair and clothing together and say "Lord of love grant me my desire" Repeat this ritual every Wednesday evening until successful.

Advice on Practical Astral Projection
Astral Projection may be described as the ability to send out the spirit from the physical body. The spirit is called the astral body and it is an exact duplicate of the physical body, but it is a much less dense form and it is nearly always invisible, thought its presence may be felt or seen occasionally. The astral body is the seat of the consciousness and responds instantly to direct thought.

The astral body is thought to leave the physical body during sleep and hover over it. Both Bodies are connected during the life of the physical body by a solver cord that can be stretched to infinity. This silver cord is the means of communication between the two bodies and is only broken on death when the astral body remains upon the astral plane until it moves onto a higher plane.

The astral body is controlled by thought. Once you have mastered the technique of astral projection you may travel anywhere you please in the world simply by wishing yourself to be there. Therefore great care and discipline of the mind is necessary to prevent yourself going inadvertently to some unpleasant place where you may not be welcome by malevolent entities that may gather there, such as an old haunted house.

It is generally thought that most people project astrally during sleep and visit places that they think about in their waking hours. These astral trips are only remembered as rapidly fading dreams in the morning light and by the time we are fully awake all memory of your trip on the astral is forgotten. But to remember all that happens to you on the astral plane, you must project intentionally and be in full control of your astral body and direct it where you wish to go.

Advice on how to Project
The best time for astral projection as a novice is at night when your body is as its lowest ebb and at its most relaxing time to separate from the astral body.

Go to your bedroom, lie upon your bed and close your eyes and go over the very first task you were asked to perform when you started. Allow your thoughts to come and go as they please for about ten minutes.

When you feel quite relaxed keep your eyes closed and begin deep breathing. Breathe in slowly while counting up to eight. Hold your breath for a further count of eight then breathe out slowly for a further count of eight. Do this until you feel you are rising from the bed. Don't move but keep on breathing in and out and holding your breath but at the same time see yourself in your mind's eye sitting up and getting off the bed and going down to your hall and out of the house.

You should by this time actually see the stairs as you go down and should you meet anyone on the way you will see and recognize them but they will be unaware of your presence. Walk around outside your house and look around you. Now wish yourself back upstairs in your bedroom. You will instantly return to your physical body.

It is possible to travel anywhere you wish in your astral body. But it is best to have a definite destination in mind before you start to project. Perhaps you know of some friends you would like to visit. See them in your mind's eye. See yourself flying above the houses to where they live. See yourself arriving and entering their house. Go where you wish when you find yourself inside. All astral projection begins on the mind. And it is only by constant practice that you eventually master the techniques and find yourself projected onto the astral plane.

Advice on the Subject of Phenomena Astral
Another method of astral projection if you have a strong and determined will is to will the astral from the physical. Carry out the first part of the exercise including the deep breathing technique and when you feel nicely drowsy, visualise your astral body as a faint replica of your physical body. Imagine in your mind's eye that the astral replica begins to rise into the air. Will it continue to rise. When it appears to be toughing the ceiling, visualise where you wish to be and your astral body to go there. Persevere until you succeed.

Since you can go anywhere at all in the world in your astral body, and as the astral plane is a replica of the world, a different vibrational level, if follows that you can visit those places where it is possible to gather facts and information that you can use to your advantage in your physical body.

Warning: Do not move your physical body once you have set in motion the techniques for astral travel. Physical movement will instantly prevent projection.

Also: Do not project for any evil purpose, such as revenge. Your astral body will reveal the colour of your mood. And there are many types of spirit entities on the astral plane and like attracts like. These evil entities will join you on your journey and can make it very difficult for you to return to your physical body because veil entities attracted by evil thoughts try to take over the physical body of the one to whom they are drawn.

Some Information on Voodoo and Black Magic Rites
This chart can be sued in voodoo and lack magic rites and spells.

I suggest – think only Good.

> Lord of Darkness, Prince of Night
> Grant my wish by astral light
> Let your mighty forces rise
> And work the spell I visualise

Lay your altar with a black altar cloth. Place four black candles in holders along the back of your altar. In front of these place two red candles in holders. In front of these red candles place your athame, the blade pointing away from you. In front of your athame place a small skull to the right and your chalice half filled with soot and vinegar to the left,

Your burner should have in it a fresh piece of charcoal upon which should be sprinkled when alight herb of witchgrass. Your candles should be anointed with mineral oil or wintergreen oil.

Wear your robe and your black belt, keeping the hood of your cloak up over your head. Swing your burner back and forth and visualise that which you desire. Once you have a clear picture in your mind let it fade and chant in a low voice: "Lord or Darkness..."2 etc

Warning: I seek to harm any person with black magic or voodoo spells or chants and using rites to that end can have dangerous repercussions in that should anything go wrong the desire sent forth will return and visit upon the sender tenfold the evil or destruction desired.

To protect themselves from this, black magicians burn three black candles for 48 hours after the ritual. At night they visualise themselves protected by a fiery red snake at the head and foot of their beds. Others sleep within a circle of white chalk impregnated with myrrh and juniper oil.

This is as far as I can take you. It is best to burn scented joss sticks for good results.

The Book. The Coggeshall Curse.
Rough Justice. Horrific tales of Murder.
The Bamber Murders that shocked
The Nation.
Mystery. Witchcraft. Homosexuality.

The unsolved murder mystery of Dr. Robert Jones's wife is just one case from the frightening catalogue of events that have come to be known as the Curse of Coggeshall.

With its pink-washed cottages and half-timbered houses, this affluent community on the edge of the Essex commuter belt seems to be like the idyllic picture postcard English village.

Life goes on at a sedate pace with visitors browsing in the 15 antique shops while old gossip on the autumn sunshine under the white clap-boarded clock tower in the market square.

It's a scene straight from the pages of a Miss Marple mystery…and like the famous thrillers; things here are not quite what they seem.

In the past five years, at least EIGHT people have been horribly murdered in and around this cosy semi-rural backwater.

On top of that there have been countless suicides, accidents and sex scandals.

The latest example of the curse came earlier this month when flamboyant restaurant owner almost burned to death in a bizarre domestic row at his country retreat in the neighbouring village of Alphamstone.

Fiery.

But strange and macabre things have been happening in Coggeshall for centuries.

In was here in 1651 at the spot know as Market Hill that the last witch to be burned at the stake in England went to her fiery doom.

Some say it was she who first cast the Curse of Coggeshall.

Whatever the explanation, Coggeshall seems to have had far more bad luck than any community of 4,000 odd outwardly respectable inhabitants could rationally expect.

In modern times, the curse first resurfaced in July 1983 with the baffling murder of doctor's wife Diana Jones.

Two years later it struck again when millionaire antiques dealer Wilfred Bull shot his wife Patsy in the head.

In August the same year came the horrific massacre of the Bamber family in the nearby village of Tolleshunt D'Arcy.

The grisly history continued into 1986 when 55 year old Coggeshall farmer Jimmy Bell shot his wife and then turned the gun on himself.

Four years later, when he took a mistress half his age, his new wife fled to her parent's home in Norfolk taking their 18 month old daughter with her.

In a possessive rage Bell, a former British clag pigeon shooting champion, turned up at the house armed with a shotgun.

Holiday Monday, May 5th, 1985 – Millionaire antiques dealer Wilfred Bull shot his wife Patsy, dead in their showroom…and initially tried to blame her death on intruders.

But his attempts to fake a burglary at their plush showroom in West Street, Coggeshall, failed. Eventually he admitted at the Old Bailey trial in March this year that he shot Patsy – but he claimed it was an accident.

A jury decided it was deliberate, and he was jailed for life.

THE BAMBER MASSACRE

The gun trap.

The rifle modelled here is a .22 fitted with a silencer like the murder weapon that played a key part in trapping the killer.

Bambi was only 5 ft. 7 ½ inches tall, so, how could she have fired the gun with the muzzle at her throat?

THE WHITE HOUSE FARM MASSACRE

The evil Jeremy Bamber would have been jailed months ago for the murder of the five members of his family but for the bumbling Essex police.

They decided within moments of finding the bodies that the killer was his sister, Bambi, who had then shot herself. They made no other enquiries.

This was compounded by breathtaking incompetence when police

- Handled the murder weapon with bare hands.
- Failed to find blood stained gun silencer and, when a relative discovered it, lost a hair – a vital clue – from it.
- Told the coroner it was murder and suicide and allowed three bodies to be cremated – thus loosing vital forensic evidence.

TIMETABLE OF EVENTS

Wednesday, 7th August, 1985: Bamber raised the alarm and police find five bodies at White House Farm. They are Bamber's father Nevill, his mother, June, both 61, nephews Daniel and Nicholas Caffell, six and his sister Sheila Caffell.

Thursday, 8th August: Police go to Sheila's flat in London and take letters and diaries. Her Iranian boyfriend is taken to Chelmsford police station for questioning and released.

Wednesday, 14th August: An inquest into the deaths is opened and adjourned. Permission is given for the family to make funeral arrangements.

Monday, 19th August: Funeral of June and Nevill Bamber and Sheila Caffell at St Nicholas Church, Tolleshunt D'Arcy, followed by cremation at Colchester.

Tuesday, 20th August: Twins Daniel and Nicholas are buried, laid to rest next to their mother in Highgate Cemetery.

Saturday, 7th September: Juile Mugford tells police of Bamber's "admissions".

Sunday, 8th September: Bamber is arrested at Sheila's flat 7am.

Monday, 9th September: Bamber appears at Chelmsford Magistrates' Court charged with burglary at his father's Osea Road Caravan Park. He is remanded in custody for four days.

Friday, 13th September: Bamber appears at Maldon Magistrates' Court and is released on unconditional bail until 16th October, accused of burglary.

Sunday, 29th September: Bamber is arrested by police in Dover after returning from a trip to France. He is charged with the murder of five members of his family.

Monday, 30th September: Bamber appears at Maldon Magistrates' Court and is remanded incustody for nine days.

Friday, 11th October: reopened inquest into the deaths is adjourned at Witham until Bamber's trial.

Wednesday, 7th May, 1986: Bamber is committed for trial by Maldon magistrates.

Thursday, 2nd October: Trial opens at Chelmsford Crown Court.

Tuesday, 28th October: Bamber is convicted on five counts of murder and is jailed for life.

Police Chief admits:

WE'VE LEARNED OUR LESSON

POLICE throughout Britain are being briefed to make sure there is no repeat of the blunders in the Bambi murder case.

A report on police handlings of the investigation has gone to Home Secretary Douglas Hurd.

And yesterday the Chief Constable of Essex, Robert Bunyard, said the lesson learned would be passed to all forces in Britain.

Essex police faced fierce criticism after the trial of 25 year old Jeremy Bamber last month.

Vital clues were missed because detectives assumed at the start that Bamber's sister Sheila "Bambi" Caffell killed four members of her family before shooting herself.

Fresh criticism has come from the Police Federation magazine Police, which attacks the Chief Constable's decision not to appoint an office from an outside force to probe the handling of the case.

But Mr. Bunyard called the magazine's criticism "out of sate and ill-judged".

Bamber shot his adoptive parents, his sister and her twin sons at White House Farm, Tolleshunt D'Arcy, Essex, in August last year.

He wasn't charged with the murders until six weeks later and then only after his ex-girlfriend, 22 year old Julie Mugford, told detectives he had planned them for nearly a year.

During the trial at Chelmsford Crown Court, the jury heard that a blood stained gun silencer used in the crime and other clues were uncovered by relatives who searched the murder scene after the police left.

It took two days for police to collect the silencer – and on the way to laboratory tests they lost a grey hair which had been attached to it.

The judge criticised that slip-up. And police admitted after the trial that they had been hood-winked by the killer.

Mr. Bunyard declared: "Everything is currently being done to ensure that any lessons learned from this case are passed out to the rest of the police service."

Jeremy Bamber blamed his mother for turning his sister mad, a murder trial heard today.

Bamber – who the jury earlier heard had fed marijuana to rats – also resented his mother for loving her grandsons more than him.

On the sixth day of the Bamber trial at Chelmsford Crown Court, Mrs Mary Mugford, of Scott Drive, Lexden, Colchester, claimed Bamber hated his mother.

Mrs Mugford – the mother of Bamber's ex-lover said: "Jeremy disliked his mother intensely."

"He resented his mother because she had sent him away to boarding school. And he never ever forgave her for that," she added.

BLAMING

"Apparently she was religious maniac and he always blamed her making Sheila mad," said Mrs Mugford.

Bamber denies murdering his parents, sister and her twin sons in what the prosecution claims was a bid to get his hands on £436,000 inheritance.

All five were found dead with gunshot wounds at White House Farm in Tolleshunt D'Arcy.

A few months before the killings in August last year Mrs Mugford said Bamber had told her his mother was thinking of changing her will in favour of her grandsons.

She said Bamber never spoke to his mother and his mother never showed any affection to him.

After the killings, Mrs Mugford said Bamber had wanted to sell "absolutely everything" and he did not want to keep any mementoes.

Miss. Mugford, 22, also of Scott Drive, broke down and sobbed when it was suggested she was trying to paint the blackest possible picture of Bamber to the jury.

"You are of course a very bright intelligent young woman." Said Geoffrey Rivlin, QC, who is defending Bamber.

"You don't wish to miss any opportunity whatsoever, do you, to make your evidence sound as black as ever possible for Jeremy?"

ADMIT

She replied, "No, again I would like to correct you here, I am telling you only what he has told me.

"The evidence is black and without me adding anything. He knows that and I know that but he knows that he can't admit that."

"He told me, I believed him."

"I don't like saying any of it – I hate it." Added Miss. Mugford. "He told me I am telling you."

How Bamber wept for dead relatives.

Jeremy Bamber burst into tears when a policeman told him his mother, father, sister and two nephews had been found dead at White House Farm.

Sgt. Christopher Bews told the jury he had broken the news to Bamber.

"He didn't make any reply. He just shut his eyes and started to cry." He said.

Bamber joined police at White House Farm in the early hours on 7th August, 1985.

He had earlier phoned them to say he had received a call from his father saying his sister Sheila had gone berserk and was threatening to kill everyone.

Sgt. Bews said his car overtook Bamber's on the way to the farm. He estimated Bamber was driving no faster than 30mph.

When Bamber did get to the farm, Sgt. Bews noticed that he did not seem upset.

"He didn't seem overly excited. It was a normal conversation as I would have with anybody.

While police waited outside the house, Bamber told them there were guns – including a loaded .22 rifle – indoors.

Bamber was asked: "Is your sister likely to go berserk with a gun?"

He allegedly replied: "She is a nutter, she has been having treatment."

Sgt. Bews added Bamber had admitted how he and his sister did not get on, saying, "I don't like her and she doesn't like me."

THE WHITE HOUSE FARM MASSACRE

Jeremy Bamber admitted getting in and out of the White House Farm secretly, claimed prosecutor Anthony Arlidge.

"Jeremy Bamber had told his girlfriend that he had found ways of getting in and out of that house without anybody apparently being able to detect it," he said.

Scientists examined a window frame to a ground floor bathroom and spotted scrapes on the paintwork as if something had been pushed in the frame.

A search outside revealed a hacksaw blade.

"The scratches on the blade matches the scratches on the catch to the window," said Mr. Arlidge.

FORCE

The blade also had paint on it which was the same as that on the window frame.

The Home Office scientist concluded that blade "had been used to force the clasp of the window open, obviously to enable someone to get in."

Mr. Arlidge Added: "During interviews Jeremy Bamber said that there were occasions when he got into the house by manipulating catches or windows, including that window."

"These events were all particularly significant because as you will hear the defendant indicated to his girlfriend he knew these two ways of getting in and out of the house.

MURDERED FOR A MILLION

Evil Jeremy Bamber was locked up last night – his dream of becoming a millionaire gone forever.

He stood to inherit the lion's share of the £600,000 family fortune and hopes it would quickly grow to a million. Now he gets nothing…except the £2.33 a week he can pick up working on a prison farm.

Bamber was in line for the wealth built up by his 61 year old adopted parents and his 95 year old grandmother who died a few months after the farmhouse massacre.

He planned to set himself up as the country squire – dividing his time between the family farms in Essex and his grandmother's "stockbroker belt" home in Guilford, Surrey.

The calculating killer reckoned to take over his family's seaside caravan park.

He was also after the tenancy of his parents' farm in addition to the $436,000 left in their wills.

That money alone clocked up an extra £100 a day in interest throughout the 12 months Bamber was in prison awaiting trial.

Pale.

But the killer's crimes have cost him any claim on the estate which will now go to relatives.

The family are spread throughout the Essex farming community. And lawyers will have to decide how the money is shared.

It took the jury nine hours and 24 minutes to reach their majority verdict yesterday.

There were gasps as the foreman said "Guilty" five times over.

Bamber looked pale. But not a flicker of emotion crossed his face as he stood erect in the crumpled blue suit he wore every day during the three week trial.

The judge told him:
"You killed your mother, father, sister and two little boys. Each would have been a dreadful crime. But you killed them all, firing shot after shot into them…..
I find it difficult to foresee whether it will ever be safe to release into the community someone who can kill five members of their own family and shoot two little boys asleep in their bed. My recommendation is that your serve a minimum of 25 years."

Blame.

Bamber used his sister Sheila's madness as a cover for the killings and rigged the evidence to put the blame on her.

The judge said, "You killed out of arrogance in your character which made you resent any form of parental control or criticism.
You wanted to be the complete master of you own life, to enjoy an inheritance which would have come to you in the fullness of time."

Essex farmer Jeremy Bamber, who is accused of murdering five members of his family, stood to inherit an estate of more that £400,000 if they died, Chelmsford Crown Court was told today.

His parents Nevill and June, sister Sheila and twin nephews Daniel and Nicholas Caffell, were shot at the Bambers' family home at White House Farm, Tolleshunt D'Arcy.

Mr. Anthony Arlidge, QC, prosecuting, said local magistrate Nevill Bamber and his wife had a joint estate valued at about £436,000.

Under the terms of their wills, 25 year old Jeremy of Head Street, Goldhanger, was the principal beneficiary from Nevill's will and Sheila from June's was a proviso that if Sheila or Jeremy died before their parents, their own children would inherit.

Mr. Arlidge said there was no evidence that Jeremy Bamber had seen the correct, legally drawn up wills, but it was clear he had seen a rough draft.

When asked by police if he knew he would inherit if Sheila and his parents died, he replied, "Understandably so", said Mr. Arlidge.

FARMHOUSE

"The picture in his mind was that if his parents and sister and two twin sons had died he would effectively inherit from the estate," said Mr. Arlidge.

Nevill Bamber was shot, beaten unconscious with a blunt instrument the "finished off" with four bullets in the head, the jury heard.

His wife was shot first in her bed and again as she walked away, apparently to get to a phone.

Mr. Bamber's injuries showed that he had tried to defend himself from the blows of a blunt instrument. After being shot in the body then beaten ne had been "carefully and calculatedly shot in the head.

Upstairs in the bedroom were found the twins dead in their beds, and two more bodies – of June Bamber and Sheila Caffell – in Mr. and Mrs Bamber's bedroom.

CANNABIS

Mrs Bamber had seven gunshot wounds, which suggested she was shot in her bed and then again as she walked away.

Sheila Caffell had two gunshot wounds, and was lying with the gun and empty magazines on top of her.

Tests later showed that she had taken cannabis a few days earlier, and had recently taken a tranquiliser. June Bamber's bible was found by Sheila's body.

A total of 25 bullets were fired the night the family died. That would have meant that the rifle being reloaded at least twice, said Mr. Arlidge.

The six year old twins, Daniel and Nicholas, were shot as they slept.

Mr. Arlidge said police had broken into the house through the scullery door four house after the phone call from Jeremy.

They found the kitchen in "considerable disarray" after an obvious struggle or fight.

Nevill Bamber was found under a mantelpiece. He had been beaten six o seven times with a blunt instrument, and it looked as if something like a rifle had been swung about the room.

There were bits of rifle butt on the floor, a lampshade was on the floor and his watch was found underneath a rug covered in his blood.

I'M EVIL, HE SAID

Greedy Romed Jeremy Bamber lusted after men, women, money and drugs. He had a huge appetite for sex and once admitted: "I am evil. I just can't stop having evil thoughts."

To the parents who adopted him as a baby, he was the spoilt son and heir who would eventually take over the family farm.

But Bamber hated his parents, loathed farming and couldn't wait to get his hands on the family fortune.

He would drive around the farm on a tractor in a haze of cannabis smoke. He wore gloves while working so he wouldn't soil his hands.

Fast cars and women were more his style. There were homosexual affairs.

Wine bar boss, Malcolm Waters, said: "Jeremy loved to camp it up, and I know of at least one male love affair"

And there were drugs – including jet-set favourite, cocaine.

Heroin.

A girl who was close to him even suggested he was involved in drug dealing.

"Jeremy told us of how he smuggled heroin from Asia to Australia," she said, "I don't believe it was for his own use because I don't think he ever took heroin. He was simply a heavy cannabis user although on occasions he did snort cocaine."

Lurking in the background of Bamber's wild life was his close friend, New Zealand, Brett Collins.

Two days after the funerals of his victims Jeremy flew to Amsterdam with Collins and his girlfriend Julie Mugford.

Bamber was there to shop for drugs. He returned to England with cannabis packed into dozens of toothpaste tubes.

He and Collins often teamed up for horseplay and after the farmhouse massacre they turned up one night at Stringfellows night club in London where they drank pink champagne and tried to pick up girls.

Jeremy and Collins flirted together – especially when they were with Bamber's girlfriend Julie Mugford.

"Brett loathed Julie and made it very clear," said one friend.

London-born Jeremy's real parents were a city accountant and a girl who became a nurse. Like his sister Sheila joined the Bamber family through the Church of England Adoption Society.

But unlike Sheila, he wasn't interested in finding out who his real parents were.

Bamber left school at 17 to work on the 750-acre family farm.

Every evening after leaving the fields, he would head for the singles bar in Colchester.

TRAGEDY OF THE MODEL

GLAMOUR girl Sheila tried desperately to be a top model. She failed and slipped into drugs. A relative said: "She found herself unable to cope with the artificial world of modelling. She became a casualty of the permissive society."

MODEL'S BROKEN DREAMS

REDHEAD Bambi Caffell craved stardom as a model. But she wasn't really cut out for the tough competitive world of modelling.

Bambi worried constantly about her looks and even had her breasts enlarged.

She did a Bacardi Rum advert – appearing long distance on a beach because sunburn on fair skin ruled out a close-up.

Later the struggling model did soft porn pictures for men's magazines.

Too ashamed to tell her husband about the nude photos, she consulted her best friend on whether her stretch marks were obvious and should be hidden under suspenders and stockings.

Jeremy Bamber got hold of the pictures. And in a final act of contemptuous betrayal, he tried to sell them after her death.

Jeremy's pay rise.

Shortly after the death of his family, Jeremy Bamber gave himself a pay rise.

Bamber gave himself £75 a week extra because he had more responsibility.

Farm secretary Barbara Wilson, who dealt with the wages, said Bamber told her he was to have more money.

'Jeremy never hit sister'

The housekeeper at White House Farm told the jury she had never heard Jeremy utter a bad word about his family in more than 20 years.

"You have never heard Jeremy say anything nasty about his parents, have you?" asked Geoffrey Rivlin QC, who is defending Bamber.

"No, not me", replied Jean Bouttell, who has worked at the farm for 20 years.
"Or about his sister, or his nephews?" asked Mr. Rivlin.
"No."
"You have known him long enough, haven't you?" added Mr. Rivlin.
"Yes" Replied Mrs Bouttell.
"And you have never seen him show and violence towards his sister, even when they were little?" Mrs Bouttell said she had not.

She told the court Mrs June Bamber had been a very religious woman.

THE MAN accused of the Bambi murders strangled rats with his bare hands to see if he could kill his family that way, his jilted lover claimed yesterday.

"He thought of several ways of getting rid of them" Julie Mugford told the jury.

He considered drugging their drinks and burning the house down. Then he remembered there was some valuable silver which was not insured, she said.

Miss. Mugford, 22, told Chelmsford Crown Court that she protested. "These were pretty vile things to say and I'd rather he didn't speak to me about it, it was horrible"

Bamber denies murdering his adoptive parents, both 61, his sister, model Sheila "Bambi" Caffell, 27 and her twin six year old sons Nicholas and Daniel.

They were all found dead at the family home. Whitehouse Farm, Tolleshunt D'Arcy, Essex, on August 7th last year.

JEREMY BAMBER grew marijuana on his father's farm, his jilted girlfriend told the Bambi murder trial yesterday.

Julie Mugford said Bamber was able to catch rats and strangle them with his bare hands because they had been eating the drug.

She told of a joke Bamber made about the rats "Jeremy was laughing because they had eaten his marijuana. He said it had slowed them down and that was how he caught them," she said.

Earlier she said he strangled the rats to test his will to kill.

Miss Mugford, 22, told Chelmsford Crown Court that Bamber frequently smoked the drug. She did so occasionally.

Bamber, 25, denies shooting his adoptive parents Nevill and June Bamber, both 61, his sister Sheila "Bambi" Caffell and her twin sons.

Julie began sobbing as the defence lawyer accused her of "trying to make the evidence as black as possible for Jeremy"

Gesturing furiously at Bamber in the dock, Julie said, "I am only telling you what he told me. I don't like it – I hate it"

Miss. Mugford left the court in tears at the end of her evidence, after spending five hours in the witness box over two days.

Later her mother, Mrs Mary Mugford, said Bamber felt bitter hatred for his adoptive mother because she sent him to boarding school.

"He never forgave her for that. He couldn't see why you should adopt someone and then send them away" She said.

Mrs Mugford said she and Bamber got on very well. He called her "mummy" and referred to himself as her favourite son-in-law.

Bamber told police he did not speak to his mother. "I couldn't understand it and I thought it was very strange" she said.

List

"After the murders he offered me his mother's small car. He said he was drawing up a list and that he was going to sell everything from the house. He wanted no mementos, nothing at all. He wanted to sell it" she said.

Plumber Matthew MacDonald denied to the jury that he was the hitman who killed the Bambers.

Miss. Mugford had claimed that Bamber told her he gave MacDonald £2,000 to commit the murders.

But Mr. MacDonald said he and some friends spent the night of the murders with Mrs Mary Southgate.

JEREMY BAMBER was plotting to commit the perfect murder of his parents a year before they died; it was alleged at Chelmsford Crown Court.

His original plan was to put a sleeping drug in the drinks, shoot them and then set fire to their home, White House Farm, Tolleshut D'arcy, making it look as though his father had fallen asleep while smoking, said Anthony Arlidge, QC, prosecuting.

He had even practiced with his girlfriend's tranquilisers to see what effect they would have with drink.

But he abandoned the plan when he discovered the house and its contents were under-insured. He feared a valuable clock would be destroyed too.

HARLOT

Bamber's scheme to commit the perfect murder will be told by his former girlfriend Julie Mugford, when she gives evidence to the Court, the jury was told yesterday, when Bamber denied murdering his father Nevill, mother June, sister Julie Caffell and her twin sons Nicholas and Daniel.

But in his opening speech Mr. Arlidge outlined what Julie Mugford will say.

He told her he had paid a friend Matthew MacDonald £2,000 to kill the family. Sheila had shot herself on Mr. MacDonald's orders.

But Mr. Arlidge said Mr. MacDonald says he had nothing to do with the killings and was with a girlfriend at the time.

SUFFERING

Bamber went on a spending spree, but his girlfriend's loyalty to him became strained, and the guilt of her knowledge "began to weigh on her", said Mr. Arlidge.

"He said he has no feelings about the killings and agreed if he was like that, there must be something wrong with him," he said, "She told him she must be suffering for both of them"

The two separated after a quarrel and a fight and Julie went to the police with her story on 7th September – a month after the shootings.

When she had threatened earlier to tell the police, Bamber said because she had hidden what he had done, she was implicated.

Mr. Arlidge pointed out that in law in would not matter whether Bamber had personally shot them or arranged for someone else to shoot them on his behalf.

It would still be murder.

The case continues.

New life abroad for his former girlfriend Julie.

THE prosecution's key witness in the case against Jeremy Bamber was his scorned girlfriend Julie Mugford. He had once asked her to marry him.

But she was outraged when she discovered he had slept with her friend.

The relationship was over. She said she could bear the burden of knowing his crime no longer and she went to the police.

Julie was a successful student, attending Colchester County High School for Girls until 1982 before studying for a degree in education at Goldsmiths College, London University.

She said his first plot was to drug them with his mother's tranquillisers and then set fire to the house.

She went to Witham police station a month after the family's deaths because, she said, she could not stand the burden any longer.

In the witness box, however, she said she still loved him.

Her story was endorsed by Jeremy's uncle Robert Boutflour who told the Court Jeremy had said he could kill.

Mr. Bamber's lawyer Geoffrey Rivlin, QC, claimed Julie Mugford had made up the tale of the plot because she was jilted.

She denied it and her evidence was damning.

SHOCKED
Te jury believe her and Bamber was jailed for life for the crime.

Speaking from jail before the appeal, he said he remembered being shocked and stunned at her story to the Court.

In the list that really means life.

JEREMY Bamber is prisoner L12373

The L denotes the fact that he has been ordered to serve a life sentence after he was convicted of the White House Farm murders.

In 1997, Jeremy Bamber was put on a list of prisoners who would never be released from jail.

Other on the list included the Yorkshire Ripper, Peter Sutcliffe, the Moors murderers Myra Hindley and Ian Brady and House of Horrors killer Rosemary West.

Bamber has encountered some of Britain's most notorious criminals during his 17 years in jail.

At Whitemoor high security prison in Cambridgeshire he has met:

Barry George, jailed for life for the murder of TV presenter Jill Dando.

Michael Steele, 55, of Great Bentley, dubbed the Angel of Death. Steele was convicted for the gangland killings of Tony Tucker, Pat Tate and Craig Rolfe at Rettendon in December 1995.

Jack Whomes, 36, of Brockford, Suffolk, also jailed for life for the Rettendon murders.

Dennis Nilson, 54, the civil servant jailed for life in 1983 for six murders and two attempted murders, having killed and dismembered 15 men.

Pair was adopted as babies.

Bath Jeremy Bamber and Sheila Caffell were adopted as babies from the Church of England.

One of the society's rules of adoption was that the children had to be told of their background by a certain age.

Jeremy and Sheila had been told since they were about seven that they were adopted. As they approached adulthood, their adoptive parents June and Nevill told them they could contact the adoption agency to find out who their natural parents were.

Jeremy chose not to, but Sheila chose to find out.

Sheila's natural mother turned out to be the daughter of Canon Eric Jay, senior chaplain to the then Archbishop of Canterbury.

Her father was a curate and it had been decided that Sheila would be put up for adoption with the church society.

Sheila found out who her mother was and corresponded with her.

They also met in May 1985, just three months before the killings but were never to meet again.

Apology to relatives over the Bamber mistakes.

The top policemen in Essex has met murderer Jeremy Bamber's remaining relative to apologise for the way detectives ignored vital evidence they uncovered.

Chief Constable Robert Bunyard had lunch and a long meeting at police headquarters in Chelmsford with the Boutflour family, who turned amateur detective after the White House Farm massacre.

Bamber's uncle Robert Boutflour and cousins David Boutflour and Ann Eaton found a blood-stained silencer and other clues which had been overlooked by detectives at the Tolleshunt D'Arcy farmhouse.

These proved vital in the case against 25 year old Jeremy Bamber, who was jailed for life for the five murders, but is hoping to appeal against the verdict.

Mr. Bunyard confessed: "Regrettably the senior investigators did not appreciate the significance of the information which was supplied to them and consequently failed to take appropriate action as early as they could have done.

"We could have given more weight to what the family was telling us, and because we didn't I have apologised to them"

Speaking after a meeting of Essex police committee on Monday, Mr. Bunyard revealed that important lessons had been learned from the mistakes.

He said senior policemen had been told they must keep an open mind and important investigations were now discussed in the presence of an officer not directly involved in the collection of evidence.

"He can give an impartial view and verdict of cases he hears discussed," said Mr. Bunyard, who added the officer would be acting as "devil's advocate".

After the farmhouse murders, police immediately assumed Bamber's sister, Sheila Caffell, had shot her parents and twin sons because of the way the scene had been arranged.

Mr. Bunyard also revealed that he would be pressing Her Majesty's Inspector of Constabulary – who is probing the Essex police handling of the murders for Home Secretary Douglas Hurd – for increased help from scientific experts.

"The officers at the scene did not have the benefit of advice from scientific experts," he pointed out.

Ballistic experts may have been able to give indications about the trajectory of bullets.

A biologist could have shed light in the order of the shots, and it would have been beneficial to have had a forensic pathologist examine bodies before they were removed.

A JUDGE today criticised the police over the handling of a vital piece of evidence in the Bamber massacre investigations.

The reprimand same when a top fingerprint expert agreed there had been errors.

And he agreed that police were convince that Sheila Caffell had blasted her parents and twin sons to death before turn the gun on herself.

Jeremy Bamber, 25, of Head Street, Goldhanger, denied murdering his adoptive parents, sister and her twin sons in a bid to inherit the family £436,000 estate.

Under cross examination by Bamber's defence barrister, Geoffrey Rivlin, QC, Det. Insp. Ronald Cook told a Chelmsford Crown Court jury that a silencer – which had been attached to the murder weapon – was only found six days after the killings.

FOUND

And Det. Insp. Cook admitted that he had not looked in a cupboard during a search of the murder house where the silencer was eventually found.

"I could have done if I had a reason," said Det. Insp. Cook.

He also admitted he had failed to tell the forensic science laboratory that there was a grey hair on the silencer.

Det. Insp. Cook said the hair had later become detached from the silencer, and he admitted he had not bothered to search his car for it.

At this point, trial judge Mr. Justice Drake, said the forensic laboratory "should have been told" to expect the hair.

He said they could have looked for it in the packaging around the silencer.

But Dep. Insp. Cook said he was only aware that it had "limited evidential value".

Mr. Rivlin also asked why police touched the Rifle used in the massacre without wearing gloves.

Dep. Insp. Cook admitted gloves were available on the day the five bodies were found at the White House Farm in Tolleshunt D'Arcy.

The jury of seven men and five women heard how fingerprint tests were eventually made on the 22. Rifle used in the slaughter.
The fingerprint of Bamber's right forefinger was found going across the breach of the barrel.

The Court heard his fingerprints were only tested about 11 weeks after the killing.

The mark of Sheila Caffell's right ring finger was found on the stocks of the gun, added Det. Insp. Cook.

The jury was also told how a bible, which was found in the bedroom, by Sheila Caffell, was tested.
Most marks found on it belonged to Mrs Bamber, said Det. Insp. Cook.

But another clear print speared to have been made on the bible by a child.

No fingerprint tests were ever carried out on the bodies of Sheila Caffell's twins Nicholas and Daniel, 6, admitted Det. Insp. Cook.

Day he ordered an office clearout.

JEREMY BAMBER ordered his father's office to be cleared out – as he did not want anything that reminded him of his father.

Farm secretary Barbara Wilson told the jury Bamber's manner was "arrogant and nasty"

"He came up to the office and said he wanted everything thrown out and didn't want anything left", said Mrs Wilson.

WARNED

Under cross examination, Mrs Wilson insisted Bamber had been arrogant.

"When someone comes upstairs, sits in the chair, outs his feet on the desk and swivels round and tells me in the manner he told me to clear things out, I am not mistaken," she said.

Earlier the Court heard Jeremy had warned police he did not want anything stolen if they searched the farmhouse.

Det. Insp. Robert Miller asked Bamber if police could go to the farm on the evening of 14th August – a week after the massacre.

"Det. Insp. Jones, who was also present, asked him not to say things like that, to which he replied "I was only joking"

Jeremy Bamber was arrested but then release by police, the jury heard.

Barbara Wilson, the Bamber's secretary for seven years, said she found a note in her office from Jeremy "after he had been released following his arrest."

The note simple said: "Barbara, pay all my solicitors' fees," she recalled.

The Bamber Murders

What is there if any way to describe the horrific murder of a whole family. Gone seem to be the days of one isolated murder. Recently there have been reports of mass murders. People in their village are still shocked by it all. How safe are the people today? Are the police the guardians we expect them to be: do the police blunder? This is no first time Essex police have blundered in a major murder. The Barn murder was a bit of a hiccup. Mistakes will always be made; the lesson is in their language.

The police have a very difficult job at times. The respect that you expect cannot be bought, neither can friendship be bought. Lies are more often believed than truth.

These recent cases are not natural. On of the senior Essex police officers involved in the Bamber enquiry fell from a ladder whilst off duty painting his house, and died.

Society and people are changing fast – a new breed is developing. Contract and hit men seem to be with us. It's a long way from your caring village policeman and some so care: they are family men with friends. After all, you have to turn to someone for help in times of distress. The role of a policeman in society cannot be replaced. Someone once said, "Not only must justice be done, but it also has to be seen to be done".

Jeremy Bamber was found guilty by an English jury. How can you disregard anything? One prosecution witness said a hit man was hired. It is a tragic, unnatural case. What did happen? I have collected articles on what some people said.

It was first thought that Sheila Caffell killed the family, and then committed suicide. However, the case took a different twist when fresh evidence was produced.

The contents of this case are quite horrifying – the verdict was guilty. Read for yourself the awful tragedy of an Essex family. If mistakes were made, who made them – was the guilty verdict a just one?

The Five Charges

Jeremy Bamber, 25 at the time, a farmer of Head Street, Goldhanger, denied murdering his adoptive parents, Nevill and June Bamber – both 61 – their daughter Sheila Caffell, 27, and her twin sons Nicholas and Daniel, 6, at the family home, White House Farm, Tolleshunt D'Arcy, near Maldon, Essex, in August 1985. Flanked by police office he answered, "Not guilty" in a slow, clear voice when the charges were read…..

Bamber Case to Start at Crown Court

The story of the Essex farmhouse massacre, which shocked the nation, unfolded to a jury at Chelmsford Crown Court. The just heard how bodies of two little boys, their mother and grandparents, were found with fatal bullet wounds at the Bamber family's Tolleshunt D'Arcy farm. Before them will be farmer Jeremy Bamber, accused of murdering five members of his family. He is alleged to have killed his adoptive father Nevill, adoptive mother June, sister Sheila Caffell and her twin sons Nicholas and Daniel at White house Farm – Nevill and June's isolated home.

Jeremy Bamber, 25, of Head Street, Goldhanger, had been in custody for a year, following his arrest, six weeks after the five bodies were found. Nevill and June Bamber, both 61, their adopted daughter Sheila, 27, and her six year old sons were found dead in the house on august 7th, 1985. They were found by police who broke into White House Farm after armed officers surrounded it for three hours.

Nevill Bamber had farmed there for many years, and had been magistrate on the Witham bench for the last 25.

He was a tireless worker for the village, as was his wife June, who was devoted to her family, and worked hard for the church. Their daughter Sheila, who had modelled professionally under the name Bambi, was recently divorces, and lived in London, but was a regular visitor to her parents' farm.

Ralph Nevill Bamber
Age:61. Occupation: Farmer. Background: Wealthy tenant farmer of White House Farm, Tolleshunt D'Arcy, magistrate, church warden; former parish councillor.

June Bamber
Age: 61. Occupation: Farmer's wife Background: Warden at St. Nicholas Church, Tolleshuunt D'Arcy; connected with village horticultural society and Women's Institute; collector for the Church of England Children's Society.

Daniel and Nicholas Caffell
Age: 6 Background: Identical twin sons of Sheila Caffell, only grandsons of Nevill and June Bamber. In their short lives they had know unhappiness, but towards the end Sheila Caffell's twins were wrapped in the simple joys of childhood. Six year old Kicholas and Daniel went to stay with their father when their mother could no longer cope. Then Sheila took the excited youngsters to stay with their loving grandparents. They played happily around the farm. The long summer evenings would end with bedtime stories.
The twins were sleeping, their thumbs in their mouths, when their uncle crept into their room and shot them through the head.

Jeremy Bamber
Age: 25. Occupation: Farmer. Background: Lived in Head Street, Goldhanger; shareholder of Osea Road Caravan Site, Heybridge; employee of his father; adopted son of Nevill and June Bamber; accused of murdering Mr. and Mrs Bamber, his sister Sheila Caffell and her sons Nicholas and Daniel.

Sheila "Bambi" Caffell
Age: 37. Occupation: Former fashion model. Background: Adopted daughter of Nevill and June Bamber; mother of six year old twins Nicholas and Daniel; recently divorced; lived in Maida Vale, London.
Glamour girl Sheila tried desperately to be a top model. She failed and slipped into drugs. A relative said: "She found herself unable to cope with the artificial world of modelling. She became a casualty of the permissive society." Redhead Bambi Caffell craved stardom as a model. But she wasn't cut out of the tough competitive world of modelling. Bambi worried constantly about her looks and even had her breasts enlarged. She did a Bacardi rum advert – appearing long distance on a beach because sunburn on her fair skin ruled out a close-up.
Later the struggling model did soft porn pictures for men's magazines. Too ashamed to tell her husband about the nude photos, she consulted her best friend on whether her stretch marks were obvious and should be hidden under suspenders and stockings. Jeremy Bamber got hold of the pictures. And in a final act of contemptuous betrayal, he tried to sell them after her death.

Curse of the Murder Mansion
Twice before has the Bamber farmhouse been the scene of a tragedy. The man who it before the Bambers farmer Frank Page, was found drowned in a horse trough in 1946. The owner before him hanged himself. Now the "250,000 red brick farmhouse at Tolleshunt D'Arcy stands empty. Housekeeper, Mrs Jean Boutell, who called there every day to clean and dust said: "Sometimes I wonder if there's a curse on the place, it's seen so much tragedy it might be better if they bulldozed it".

The Dog that had to Die
As the killer rampaged through the Bamber farmhouse, Crispy the dog took refuge under a bed. The cowering two year old grey and white terrier was taken to Jeremy Bamber's cottage in a nearby Goldhanger by police. It repeatedly tried to bite him, so he had it put down.
Farm Manager, Jeremy Bamber was close to tears in the witness box at Chelmsford Crown Court, as he told a jury of the night five members of his family died. Bamber denied he was responsible for the killings and claimed his former girlfriend had made accusation against him out of spite following

the break-up of their relationship. The prosecution alleged that Bamber carried out the killings in a bid to inherit £436,000.

Bamber denied murdering his adoptive parents June and Nevill, his sister and her twin sons. Bamber described how he left the farmhouse after leaving his father's .22 rifle, which he had used to hunt rabbits, leaning against a kitchen wall. The rifle was unloaded, but the magazine was nearby.

Early next morning he received phone call from his father saying," Sheila has gone crazy – she has got a gun". He added: "I don't remember the exact words. It just ended after that. There was no more. I didn't have a chance to say a word. It just went dead. I telephoned back two or three times. It was engaged each time. Then I called the police".

Bamber said he rang Chelmsford police station but the officer did not seem to take him seriously until the end of a five minute conversation. The court heard that Bamber was arrested a few weeks later after his girlfriend Julie Mugford told police he had told her he had arranged for a mercenary to carry out the killings for £2,000.

But in evidence, Bamber denied ever telling Miss Mugford he had hired a mercenary or had given her a description of what happened at the farmhouse. He said she had lied in the witness box. Under cross examination Bamber denied killing his family and trying to make it appear that his sister had done so and then committed suicide.

Earlier, Mr. Geoffrey Rivlin, QC, defending, told members of the jury they would have to consider Sheila Caffell's metal state on the night her family was murdered. He said she suffered from a major mental disorder which resulted in her losing her grip on reality. She thought she was a white witch and that she was increasingly being taken over by the devil.

The Call for Help
Jeremy Bamber phones two police stations – in Chelmsford and Witham, rather than dialling 999 on the night of the killings, it is alleged. He claimed he could get no reply from Witham, so he called Chelmsford instead. The Phone call to Chelmsford police station was first logged at 3.36am – more than half an hour after he called his girlfriend to say something was wrong.

Secret Ways In and Out of the Farmhouse
Jeremy Bamber admitted getting in and out of White House Farm secretly, claimed prosecutor Anthony Arlidge. Jeremy Bamber also told his girlfriend that he had found ways getting in and out of that house without anybody apparently being able to detect it, he said.

Scientific examination of a window to a ground floor bathroom spotted scrapes on the paintwork as if something had been pushed inside the frame. A search outside revealed a hacksaw blade. The scratches on the blade matched the scratches on the catch to the window, said Mr. Arlidge.

The blade also had paint on it which was the same as that on the window frame. The Home Office scientist concluded the blade had been used to force the clasp of the window open, obviously to enable someone to get in. Mr. Arlidge added: during interviews Jeremy Bamber had said that there were occasions when he had got into the house by manipulating catches or windows, including that window. These events were all significant because as you will hear the defendant indicated to his girlfriend he knew these two ways of getting in and out of the house.

How Bamber Wept for Dead Relatives
Jeremy Bamber burst into tears when a policeman told him his mother, father, sister and two nephews had been found dead at White House Farm. Sgt. Christopher Bews told the jury how he broke the news to Bamber. "He didn't make any reply. He shut his eyes and started to cry", he said. Bamber joined police at White House Farm in the early hours of August 7th 1985. He had earlier phoned them to say he had received a call from his father saying his sister Sheila had gone berserk and was threatening to kill everyone.

Sgt. Bews said his car overtook Bamber's on the way to the farm. He estimated Bamber was driving at no more than 30mph. When Bamber did get to the farm, Sgt. Bews noticed he did not seem upset. "He didn't seem overly excited. It was a normal conversation as I would have with anybody."

While police waited outside the house, Bamber told them there were guns – including a loaded .22 rifle – indoors. Bamber was asked: "Is your sister likely to go berserk with a gun?" He allegedly replied: "She is a nutter – she is having treatment".

Sgt. Bews added Bamber had admitted how he and his sister did not get on, saying: "I don't like her and she doesn't like me".

Day He Ordered Office Clearout
Jeremy Bamber ordered his father's office to be cleared out – as he did not want anything that reminded him of his father. Farm secretary Barbara Wilson told the jury Bamber's manner was "arrogant and nasty". "He came up to the office and said he wanted everything thrown out and didn't want anything left", said Mrs Wilson.

Under cross examination Mrs Wilson insisted Bamber had been arrogant. "When someone comes upstairs, sits in a chair, puts his feet on the desk and swivels round and tells me in the manner he told me to clear things out, I am not mistaken," she said.

Earlier the Court heard Jeremy had warned police that he did not want anything to be stolen if they searched the farmhouse. Det. Insp. Robert Miller asked Bamber if police could go to the farm on the evening of 14th August, a week after the massacre.

Bamber made some remark about how he didn't want anything stolen, recalled Det. Insp. Ronald Cook. Det. Sgt. Jones, who was also present, asked him not to say things like that, to which he replied: "I was only joking". Jeremy Bamber was arrested, but then released by police, the jury heard.

Barbara Wilson, the Bamber's secretary for seven years, said he found a note in her office from Jeremy after he had been released following his first arrest. The note simply said, "Barbara, pay my solicitors fees", she recalled.

Jeremy Never Hit Sister
The housekeeper at White House Farm told the jury she had never heard Jeremy Bamber utter a bad word about his family in more than 20 years. "You have never heard Jeremy say anything nasty about his parents, have you?" asked Geoffrey Rivlin, QC, who defended Bamber. "No, not me", replied Jean Boutell, who had worked at the farm for 20 years. "Or about his sister, or nephews?" asked Mr. Rivlin. "No". "You have know him long enough, haven't you?" added Mr. Rivlin. "Yes" replied Mrs Boutell. "And you have never seen

him show any violence towards his sister, even when they were little?" Mrs Boutell said she had not. She told the Court Mrs June Bamber had been a very religious woman. She said there were a number of bibles in the house, and one was normally kept beside Mrs Bamber's bed. She said Mrs Bamber sometimes used to leave notes about the bible around the house.

Jeremy's Pay Rise
Shortly after the death of his father, Jeremy Bamber gave himself a pay rise. Bamber gave himself £75 a week extra because he had more responsibility. Farm secretary Barbara Wilson, who dealt with the wages, said Bamber told her he was to have more money.

"Harlot" Taunt by Mother
The jury heard that Jeremy Bamber rowed with his mother over his relationship with a woman. June Bamber was upset about her son sleeping with Julie Mugford. "Mrs June Bamber was very deeply religious and she disapproved of the relationship between her son and Julie to the extent that she didn't like Julie living with of apparently sleeping with her son", said Anthony Arlidge, QC, prosecuting. She made her views on Julie clear, apparently at one time calling her a Harlot.

Jeremy Bamber grew marijuana on his father's farm, his jilted girlfriend told the Bambi murder trial. Julie Mugford said Bamber was able to catch rats and strangle them with his bare hands because they had been eating the drug. She told of a joke Bamber made about the rats.

"Jeremy was laughing because they had eaten his marijuana. He said it had slowed them down and that was how he caught the", she said. Earlier she said he strangled the rats to test his will to kill. Miss Mugford, 22, told Chelmsford Crown Court that Bamber frequently smoked the drug. She did so occasionally. Bamber, 25, denied shooting his adoptive parents Nevill and June Bamber, his sister Sheila "Bambi" Caffell and her twin sons.

Julie began sobbing when defence lawyers accused her of "trying to make the evidence as black as possible for Jeremy". Gesturing furiously at Bamber in the dock, Julie said: "I'm only telling you what he told me, I don't like it – I hate it".

Miss Mugford left the Court in tears at the end of her evidence, after spending five hours in the witness box over two days. Later her mother, Mrs Mary Mugford said Bamber felt bitter hatred for his adoptive mother because she sent him to boarding school.

"He never forgave her for that. He couldn't see why you should adopt someone and then send them away", she said. Mrs Mugford said she and Bamber got on very well. He called her "mummy" and referred to himself as her favourite son in law. Bamber told her he did not speak to his mother. "I couldn't understand it and thought it was very strange", she said.

After the murders he offered me his mother's small car. He said he was drawing up a list and that he was going to sell everything from the house. "He wanted no mementos, nothing at all. He wanted to sell it", she said.

Plumber Matthew MacDonald denied to the jury that he was a hit man who had killed the Bambers. Miss Mugford had claimed Bamber told her he gave MacDonald £2,000 to commit the murders. But Mr. MacDonald said he and some friends spent the night of the murders with a Mrs Mary southgate.

Jeremy Bamber was plotting to commit the perfect murder of his parents a year before they died, it was alleged at Chelmsford Crown Court. His original plan was to put a sleeping drug in their drinks, shoot them and then set fire to their home, making it look as though his father had fallen asleep whilst smoking, said Anthony Arlidge, QC. He even practiced with his girlfriend's tranquilisers to see the effect they would have with drink. But he abandoned the plan when he discovered the house and its contents were under-insured. He feared a valuable clock would be destroyed too.

Bamber went on a spending spree, but his girlfriend's loyalty to him became strained, and the guilt of her knowledge "began to weigh on her", said Mr. Arlidge. "He said he had no feelings about the killings and agreed if he was like that there must be something wrong with him", he said. "She told him she must be suffering for both of them".

The two separated after a quarrel and a fight and Julie went to the police with her story on September 7th – a month after the shootings.

When she had threatened earlier to tell the police, Bamber said because she had hidden what he had done, she was implicated.

Mr. Arlidge pointed out that in law it would not matter whether Bamber had personally shot them or arranged for someone else to shoot them on his behalf. It would still be murder.

Jeremy's ex-lover claimed they a mercenary carried out the White House Farm massacre.

Speaking to the hushed Court, Miss Mugford alleged that Matthew MacDonald, a mercenary from the Far East, had phone Bamber to confirm everything had been done. Nervously she told the jury how Bamber – who denied killing his parents, sister and nephews – had been told in detail of their death. She said Matthew said he had had a bit of a struggle with Jeremy's father and that for an old man he was very strong and out up a fight. He added that, as instructed, his sister Sheila was told to lay down and shoot herself. Matthew placed a bible on her chest to make it look like she had some sort of religious mania. Miss Mugford told the Court. She said Bamber had told her MacDonald was paid £2,000 for carrying out the killings.

She said MacDonald had left the country after the shootings and had told Bamber that it would be best if he did not know where MacDonald was going.

Miss Mugford said on the night of the killings Bamber had phoned her three times. In the first conversation at 9.50 pm on Tuesday August 6th he had told her he had been thinking about the crime all day. Miss Mugford tola the jury Bamber said "it was going to be tonight or never". The second phone call was between 3 and 3.30 the next morning. He said to me: "Everything is going well. Something is wrong at the farm".

The final call had come at 5.40 am and Bamber had told her his sister had gone mad. She was told not to go to work and that a policeman would be picking her up and he would explain everything later.

She told the Court Bamber had been talking about killing his family for some months before the killings. She said Bamber told her his sister Sheila would be a good scapegoat since she had a mental illness.

Greedy Romeo who Grasped for More
Greedy Romeo Jeremy Bamber lusted after men, women, money and drugs. He had a huge appetite for sex and once admitted: "I am evil. I just can't stop having evil thoughts."

To the parents who adopted him as a baby, he was the spoilt son and heir who would eventually take over the family farm.

But Bamber hated his parents, loathed farming and couldn't wait to get his hands on the family fortune. He would drive around the farm on a tractor in a haze of cannabis smoke. He wore gloves while working so he wouldn't soil his hands.

Fast cars and women were more his style. There were homosexual affairs. Wine bar boss, Malcolm Waters, said: "Jeremy loved to camp it up, and I know of at least one male love affair"
And there were drugs – including jet-set favourite, cocaine.

A girl who was close to him even suggested he was involved in drug dealing. "Jeremy told us of how he had smuggled heroin from Asia to Australia," she said, "I don't believe it was for his own use because I don't think he ever took heroin. He was simply a heavy cannabis user although on occasion he did snort cocaine."

London-Born Jeremy's real parents were a city accountant and a girl who later became a nurse. Like his sister Sheila joined the Bamber family through the Church of England Adoption Society. But unlike Sheila, he wasn't interested in finding out who his real parents were. Bamber left school at 17 to work on the 750 acre family farm.

Every evening after leaving the fields, he would head for a singles bar in Colchester. Among the scores of women who fell for him was 29 year old Beautician Angela Greaves. Angela had a fling with the womanizer. Then came his 20 month affair with Julie Mugford, the 22 year old student teacher, who would eventually betray the killer to the police.

Mr. Anthony Arlidge, QC, prosecuting, said local magistrate Nevill Bamber and his wife June had a joint estate valued at about £436,000. Under the terms of their wills, 25 year old Jeremy of Head Street, Goldhanger, was the principal beneficiary from Nevill's will and Sheila from June's was a proviso that if Sheila of Jemery died before their parents, their own children would inherit. Mr. Arlidge said there was no evidence that Jeremy Bamber had seen the correct, legally drawn up wills, but it was clear he had seen a rough draft.

When asked by the police if he knew he would inherit if Sheila and his parents died, he replied, "Understandably so", said Mr. Arlidge.

"The picture in his mind was that if his parents and sister and two sons had died he would effectively inherit from the estate," said Mr. Arlidge.

Nevill Bamber was shot, beaten unconscious with a blunt instrument then "finished off" with four bullets in the head, the jury heard. His wife was shot first in her bed and again as she walked away, apparently to get to a phone. Mr. Bamber's injuries showed that he had tried to defend himself from the blows of a blunt instrument. After being shot in the body then beaten he had been "carefully and calculatedly shot in the head". Upstairs in the bedroom were found the twins dead in their beds, and two more bodies – of June Bamber and her daughter Sheila Caffell – in Mr. and Mrs Bamber's bedroom.

Mrs Bamber had seven gunshot wounds, which suggested she was shot in her bed and then again as she walked away. Sheila Caffell had two gunshot wounds, and was lying with the gun and empty magazines on top of her. Tests later showed that she had taken cannabis a few days earlier, and had recently taken a tranquiliser. June Bamber's bible was found by Sheila's body.

A total of 25 bullets were fired the night the family died. That would have meant that the rifle being reloaded at least twice, said Mr. Arlidge. The six year old twins, Daniel and Nicholas, were shot as they slept. Mr. Arlidge said police had broken into the house through the scullery door four hours after the phone call from Jeremy. They found the kitchen in "considerable disarray" after an obvious struggle or fight.

Neville Bamber was found under a mantelpiece. He had been beaten six or seven times with a blunt instrument, and it looked as if something like a rifle had been swung about the room. There were bits of rifle butt on the floor, a lampshade was on the floor and his watch was found underneath a rug covered in his blood.

Why "Bambi" could not be the Killer
Sheila Caffell showed no signed of having a rifle 25 times, the jury heard. For the 27 year old former models fingernails looked like they had just been manicured at a beauty salon, said Mr. Arlidge.

The .22 rifle was not an easy gun to use, and a police officer who tried the mechanism broke a nail. Mr. Arlidge also pointed out how Sheila – who had been a model know as "Bambi" – was found dead with clean, bare feet.

Whoever had been responsible had plainly been walking about the house. It does not take much to imagine what your feet would be like?" if Sheila had fired the rifle, traces of lead would have been expected to be found on her hands. She had no traces or very little traces of lead on her hands, he said. There were also no signs of oil from the gun on her nightdress. There were a whole number of things that simply did not fit in with her being responsible, said Mr. Arlidge.

Tormented Sheila "Bambi" Caffell went home to the father she loved and the mother she loathed to escape from her private hell. She had no way of knowing that the haven of White House Farm would become a death chamber for herself and four other innocents. Sheila wanted her doting father's help to settle a £40,000 cocaine debt.

There had been talk of healing old wounds. But within days, 25 shots from a .22 rifle were to blow the family's world apart.

To outsiders the massacre at the Georgian farmhouse in Essex seemed like an especially harsh divine judgement on the blameless lives of God-fearing country folk.

Sheila's wealthy father Nevill believe in the old-fashioned virtues. But Bambi and hr bible-quoting mother had a long running feud. Ten years before her violent death, Sheila was so badly hurt by her mother's sharp tongue that she never forgot or forgave.

June Bamber had caught her daughter sun bathing topless in a rape-seed field with Colin Caffell, the man she was to marry. "You are a child of Satan", stormed Mrs Bamber. She had planted the seeds of destruction in Sheila's disturbed mind.

In London cannabis and cocaine were freely available. But drugs only deepened the crisis of a young model who was slipping towards madness. Mother and daughter were both treated for breakdowns at St. Andrew's Hospital, Northampton. Sheila's twisted thoughts became peopled by enemies – the CIA, her new boyfriend, doctors, nurses, but the real enemy lay within the heart of her own family.

A blood stained silencer was found at the Bambers' home three days after police discovered five bodies there. Scientists found the blood matched Sheilas Caffell's grouping. Bamber's cousin, David Boutflour, discovered the silencer at the back of the gun cupboard. It had been wrapped in polythene and put in a box at the back of the cupboard.

It was examined by scientists. "It had paint on it and the paint matched the paint on the mantelpiece", said Mr. Arlidge.

It also had some blood on it and that blood was compared with the grouping with the various dead people the grouping of the blood matched Sheila Caffell's. It did not match any of the others.

The silencer must of got covered in blood because it had been put against the flesh of a body when a shot was fired. Mr. Arlidge said: "If Sheila Caffell shot herself, it must mean that she shot and injured herself, decided that she did not want to have the sound modulator (silencer) on, gone and putt it inside a wrapping in a box at the back of the gun cupboard and then walk upstairs and shot herself again. In human terms that wouldn't make any sense, would it?"

Sexy Suzette Ford shared endless nights of passion with the toy boy she nicknames "Jeremy Bear". Twice they planned to wed. And three times the stunning green-eyed Suzette fell pregnant – only to lose each child. But today her dashing young lover is behind bars – as the ruthless killer Jeremy Bamber, who wiped out the rest of his family in the sensational "Bambi" farmhouse massacre. "I still find it hard to believe", said Suzette, as Bamber started a life sentence for gunning down his family, that he had cunningly staged the gruesome scene to look as if Sheila had run amok with the rifle killing the others before turning the gun on herself. It was all arranged so that he could be the sort of person to do that", said Suzette, "but no I accept that he must have done it".

Tragic Sheila "Bambi" Caffell was born into a scandal that even involved the man who crowned the Queen. Her mother was the unmarried daughter of Canon Eric Jay, senior Chaplain to the archbishop of Canterbury. Her father was curate in the Archbishop's office. Their brief affair was hushed up at the time by her grandfather Mr. Jay. He played a leading part in the procession of clergymen in Westminster Abbey when the Queen was crowned by the Archbishop of Canterbury. Dr. Fisher was told of the affair and Sheila was put up for adoption through the Church of England.

But the secret remained hidden for almost 28 years – until early in 1984 when Sheila discovered the truth.
She contacted her real mother Christine, who flew to London from Canada, for an emotional reunion. Christine stayed a week before returning home. Six months later she learned of the violent death of the daughter she barely knew.

Sheila was born in Paddington, London in July 1957 to 19 year old Christine Jay. The canon, looking for a good home for his granddaughter, remembered Nevill Bamber, the pilot he has met during wartime service in the RAF.

He knew that the Bambers, who lived near his Essex home, were deeply religious and wanted to adopt children.

On February 6th, 1958, Sheila was registered as the adopted child of Nevill and June Bamber at Maldon County Court.

The canon quietly took his family off to a new life in Montreal, Canada. He became principal of the Montreal Theological College and later a university professor. Christine married a Canadian dentist. Back in Britain, Sheila grew up unaware of her background. But when she plunged to the depths of mental illness, June Bamber judged the time had come to tell her the truth. A close family friend said: "It was as if knowing the truth was contributing to her illness".

Murdered for a Million
The calculating killer reckoned to take over the family's seaside caravan park. He was also after the tenancy of his parents' farm in addition to the £436,000 left in their wills. That money alone clocked up an extra £100 a day in interest throughout the 12 months Bamber was in prison awaiting trial.

But the killer's crimes have cost him any claim on the estate which will now go to relatives. It took the jury nine hours and 24 minutes to reach their majority verdict. There were gaps as the foreman said "Guilty" five times over. Bamber looked pale. But not a flicker of emotion crossed his face as he stood erect in the crumpled blue suit he wore every day during the three week trial. The judge told him: "You killed your mother, father, sister and two little boys. Each would have been a dreadful crime. But you killed them all, firing shot after shot into them...I find it difficult to foresee whether it will ever be safe to release into the community someone who can kill five member of their own family and shoot two little boys asleep in their bed. My recommendation is that you serve a minimum of 25 years."

Underworld Links

Did the police make mistakes? Was a hit man employed? Are there missing links? This is not the first time Essex detectives have made a mistake in a murder case. A judge criticized the police over the handling of a vital piece of evidence in the Bamber case; a suspect was charged, released and cleared after being arrested concerning the Barn murder at Braintree.

The Bamber owned caravan park was used by people who were questioned about the Barn murder. Italian Tony, who was murdered, lived nearby. Strange coincidence of fate? This book is not detective work. It just shows that police, like everyone else, are not infallible. Also it has been proved that innocent people can be sent to prison for something they never did. What person could honestly plan to kill or hire killers to murder a complete family and hope to escape jail? The fact that Jeremy Bamber had all the luxuries if the jet set is not itself conclusive evidence of a family massacre. I feel jealously followed Jeremy Bamber like autumn follows summer.

Could we conclude anything from this evidence and more importantly should the jury have been shown these things to assess their relevance or importance to the case?

Did Essex Police conceal the existence of this note/letter and cloth?

By referring to the transcript of the evidence given by Paul Terzeon in the Royal Courts of Justice on 28th October 2002 matters become clearer. Paul Terzeon was the defense solicitor for Jeremy Bamber at the trial in 1986. During the appeal in 2002 he was questioned about the Bible:

Paragraph 141

Mr. Terzeon is asked to look at the photograph bundle

Q You see two photographs of the bible

A Yes

Q Now were those photographs that you ever saw at any stage in the lead p to or during the trial?

A No I never saw them

Q What was the nature of the request?

I wanted to know if there was any photographs of the Bible or if they knew at what page it was open and the belief at the time that the Bible did not exist it had been destroyed

Mr. Terzeon goes on to say that he visited Witham police station to look at the master bundle of photographs but no pictures of the Bible were available for him to view. He states that he asked police sergeant Stan Jones for photographs of the Bible but he was told there were none.

It is odd then to discover in 2002 that photographs did exist of the Bible when finally, after 17 years of asking, Essex Police handed them over to the defence prior to the appeal. Why these same photographs were not made available to Mr. Terzeon when he visited Witham police station in 1986 pre trial has yet to be explained.

At the appeal in 2002 no one seemed to notice either the note/letter of the crocheted cloth, or if they were noticed then the issue was not raised in Court. Once they were noticed in 2005, detailed research began to determine what had happened to both these items.

DC1470 PC Hammersely was the scenes of crime officer responsible for the recovery of the bible. The Stokenchurch document 59/6 is a contemporaneous crime scene log filled in by PC Hammersely as he found and logged each item he recovered from White House Farm.

White House Farm 6.00pm 8/8/85

DRH / 44 Bible on floor next to Sheila Caffell's body

There is no mention of either the note/letter or the crocheted cloth being secured with the bible of being individually tagged and recovered as separate items as should have been done. A very much more detailed log was filled out at the police station once the items from White House Farm were brought in by PC Hammersley.

This log Stokenchurch document 62/6, the major incident property register, has the bible listed as **item 410 Bible DRH / 44W/House Farm floor next to Sheila Caffell**

Found by DC1470 11.20am 9/8/85

Again there is no mention anywhere in the major incident property register of this note/letter or crocheted cloth. How was it that no entry was made in either the crime scene log or major incident property register referring to these items, as would be expected?

With no mention in any of these logs perhaps PC Hammersley makes mention of finding them in his witness statements or his pocket book? After careful reading of all his statements and his pocket book entries, no mention can be found of these items being discovered and recovered by him.

Essex police should have carried our forensic analysis on the bible, the note/letter and the crocheted cloth. However the Stokenchurch document 64/349 DI Cook's fingerprint tested on items found at White House Farm, makes no mention of the bible ever being fingerprinted. There is again no mention made of these other items being fingerprinted.

This in itself seems unusual because the Crown's case against Jeremy Bamber is that he staged the crime scene and place the bible next to Sheila Caffell. If this were true then surely they would have fingerprinted the bible to establish this as fact?

This becomes an even more compelling point when it was revealed during the 2002 appeal that there were a number of bloody fingerprints on certain page of the bible. Clearly these were not from Jeremy Bamber so who did they belong to and why have the police never produced this evidence? In the light of the bloodied fingerprints being on certain bible pages can we assume there were similar prints on the note/letter?

From the official records kept by Essex police we are expected to believe that no fingerprint examination was made of the bible or the note/letter found between its pages, yet in the light of what we know this does not spear to be credible. Perhaps DRH/44 the bible was sent for forensic analysis to Huntingdon Forensic Laboratory to asses if it had firearms residue on it or to see whose blood had made the bloody finger marks on its pages?

The Crown's case was that Jeremy Bamber had committed the killings and then stages the scene to make it appear that Sheila had done it and then committed suicide. If this were true then testing the bible for firearms residue would be very telling. If he had placed the bible next to her body after she was killed, then no firearms residue would be on it but if Sheila had it next to her prior to the suicide, then it would have firearms residue on it and that would be compelling evidence as to Jeremy Bamber's innocence. So why were these tests not carried out?

Looking at all of the booking logs at the Home Office Forensic Laboratory at Huntingdon there is no mention of the bible DRH/44 ever having been submitted for forensic investigation. All the items for submission forms have also been carefully looked at to see if Essex police submitted the bible to Huntingdon to any other forensic laboratory, but it was never submitted, which seems peculiar.

Could this note/letter be nothing more than a red herring and of no relevance to this case?

It can be seen by looking at the part protruding from the bible pages that the words **love of another** are readable. These words come from the passage in **John chapter 13** dealing with Jesus and the last supper. Because very little of this note/letter can be seen we can only speculate about its content, but **John chapter 13** has these quotes which might have some relevance:

[2] And supper being ended the devil having now put into the heart of Judas Iscariot

[9] Simon Peter saith unto him Lord not my feet only but my hands and my head (Jesus is washing his disciple's feet)

[36] Simon Peter saith unto him Lord, wither goest thou? Jesus answered him wither I go thou canst not follow me [37] now but thou shalt follow me afterwards. Peter said unto him Lord why cannot I follow thee now I will lay down my life for thy sake

It would appear that this series of passages may have been interest to the jury in 1986, especially so in the light of Dr Ferguson (Sheila's psychiatrist) stating in evidence that Sheila's mental illness was often influenced by conflicts of good and evil and the devil being in people s well as obsessing about God and religion.

It could have been assumed that Essex police would have asked Dr Ferguson prior to the trial about significance of this note/letter or the relevance of the bible pages at which it was open. In a statement dated 6th August 2002 Dr Ferguson states that he was unaware of the pages the bible was open at nor does he make mention in any statement of Essex police showing him the note/letter, so the jury had no information from any source to guide them about the importance of the bible and they were kept unaware of the existence of a possible suicide note/letter.

Why was this crocheted cloth there at all? Was it some sort of prayer cap or mantilla? Was it used to wipe hands or simply to act as a bookmark? Not only do we not know anything about the note/letter or this cloth but we don't know which pages of the bible they were between and if those passages on those pages would have any relevance.

We cannot even be sure that the photograph of the bible resting against Sheila's arm is an accurate representation of the scene as discovered by the police. In an interview with PS Adams with the Coty of London police in 1991 it states:

Photo of 'Sheila' not in same position as when I saw it (8.10am)

Head (1) too close to bedside table

- **Not sure about the angle of head but something not right**
- **No recollection of gun**
- **Bible shown next to body was level with her waist 12 – 18" away**

C Collins and I had a conversation about the position of the bible his opinion could have been there sitting up reading put it down away from body

This would appear to suggest that someone moved the bible after PS Adams and PC Collins saw it at 8.10am because when photographs after 10am, it was propping up her arms at almost shoulder height. Furthermore by looking at all of the photographs of the bible, it appears to be open at completely different pages in different photographs which would be very irregular as it would indicate someone restaging the scene between photographs.

The very fact that Essex police have kept this note/letter and crocheted cloth out of the evidence is very suspicious. If they were of no relevance to the case then why not disclose them? Why was Paul Terzeon told by Essex police that the bible had been destroyed? And why was it never fingerprinted or forensically someone else who could have killed the family – either way it was absolute proof of my innocence as I was with the police at the time of the sighting.

I am sure that these documents that continue to be withheld contain the proof that we did see a person alive in the master bedroom and that office Saxby was not prepared to alter his pocket book or Scenes of Crime Report, hence why they have always been withheld along with the Telephone Messages, Audio Recordings of the radio and telephone calls and the Firearms Register.

These alterations to the pocket books and the Telephone Log was quite effective until the police inadvertently provided us with other documents in 2004 where we were able to see the inconsistencies.

Jeremy's request to Essex Police

Jeremy's response

Essex police are wrong to state that they have complied with my Freedom of Information requests. They have not fulfilled any of my requests to them for information relating to the first five hours of the incident at White House Farm except for two documents which are not directly relevant.

On the 2nd January 2005, I wrote to them requesting information – Essex police replied on 31st January providing no documents and asking for more specific requests. In February I wrote asking for specific documents. On 31st March I wrote again asking why my previous requests had not been met. On the 15h April Essex police replied stating that they held no Firearms Register for the police officer being issued with firearms, that they have no audio recordings of the radio or telephone calls from 7th August 1985 although Mr. Bonnett stated that he made recordings of all calls. They asked for more specific names of officers that received telephone calls in order to access the Telephone Message Logs I requested.

They did however send copies of officer Myles and officer Bews pocket notebooks but crucially not officer Saxby's.

On the 17th May I wrote again with the specific requests and on the 23rd May the police sent some documents but again note of which I had asked for. Finally on the 4th July Essex police wrote back with their reasons for being unable to assist me under the Freedom of Information Act - see letter from Essex police.

Out of the 60 documents I requested I have been provided with only 2 which contain nothing of relevance. The police have sent me 12 other documents which were not requested and bore no importance whatsoever to the case. None of the remaining 58 documents have ever been seen by the defence and one had to wonder why Essex police chose to not make available all contemporaneous records made during those crucial first five hours of the incident on 7th August 1985.

The basic facts of the case are well known. At 7.35am on 7th August 1985, officers of the Essex Constabulary forcefully entered White House Farm, Tolleshunt D'Arcy. After a half-hour search they had found five bodies: those of Nevill Bamber, his wife June, their adopted 28 year old daughter, Sheila Caffell, and her twin six year old sons.

At approximately 3.15am, the Bambers' 24 year old adopted son, Jeremy, who lived in a neighbouring village, had telephones the local police, informing that his father has just 'phones, telling him that his sister, Sheila, had gone crazy and had a gun. Jeremy Bamber met police officers at the farm at about 3.40am.

The police initially believed that Sheila, who had a history of mental illness, had committed four murders before shooting herself, but member of the extended family soon set about convincing the police that Jeremy was responsible. In due course, he was arrested, charged and convicted.

The trial was unusual. The judge ruled that only Sheila or Jeremy could have committed the murders. Consequently, a major thrust of the prosecution case was to demonstrate that Sheila could not have been responsible and that Jeremy was therefore guilty. It was a near-run thing. The jury convicted Bamber on a 10:2 majority vote. If just one of the ten jurors had wavered, Bamber would have walked away a free man. Instead, he has been incarcerated for nineteen years, consistently protesting his innocence.

Subsequent developments – in particular during the last twelve months have given rise to grave concern that Bamber's conviction is another of the great miscarriages of justice in the 1980s which so marred our judicial system, to be bracketed with the Birmingham Six, the Guildford Four

Jeremy's request to Essex Police

and others. With Bamber, the key issue had been, and remains, the non-disclosure of evidence to the defence. At the time of his trial, police and prosecution were only obliged to hand other evidence which the defence requested. The deficiency is glaringly obvious: the defence could not ask for evidence and the existence of which they did not know.

Earlier in 2004, Bamber's new defence team looked at the evidence again. Exhibit 29 caught their attention: a document listing some radio messages from the scene of crime. Defence wondered if this might be the first page of a longer document rather than a complete document in itself. They sought clarification.

Essex constabulary was adamant: the one-page Exhibit 29 was a while document and had been available to the defence of the trial. Unconvinced, Bamber's defence took the matter to Court in March 2004. They were successful. The police produced the entire document. Exhibit 29, it transpired, was not a single page document. Bamber's solicitors received by fax a twenty-four page summary of radio communications.

Bamber's solicitors next took the unusual step of writing to both the trial judge and to the chief prosecution counsel, enquiring if either had known at the time of the trial of the existence of this lengthier log of radio messages. Both replied that they had not.

On receiving the twenty-four pages, the defence had immediately noticed that the first two pages had not only been re-written on different paper from the rest but they had also been edited. A comparison with police witness statements revealed that several key radio messages had been left out. Why? The defence therefore asked for the original document so it could be sent to ESDA testing. Essex constabulary refused. The request has been repeated many times; each time the constabulary has refused.

The disclosure of the radio message log was not the only dramatic development last March. Bamber's defence had requested only one document, but perhaps inadvertently, the police also provided evidence which had not been requested: pages from a contemporaneous telephone log and from a contemporaneous incident report. The defence had not known either existed.

It was immediately apparent that the radio and telephone logs and the incident report which the police had withheld contained details which were inconsistent with the case put out by the prosecution at Bamber's trial. I shall give just two examples. Others may be used by Bamber's defence on another occasion.

First, at 5.25am officers in the police car call sign CA7 (the same officers who had met Bamber at White House Farm and spent much time with him) relayed a message from the tactical firearms team to incident headquarters: "Firearms teams are in conversation with a person from inside the farm".

If the police were in conversation with someone inside the farm at 5.25am, the case against Bamber collapses. He could not have murdered everyone in the farmhouse before 3.00am if at 5.25am the police were talking to one of the supposed victims. If, on the other hand, the police were in conversation with some 'third party' inside the house, the judge's ruling that either Jeremy or Sheila and no one else committed the murders is blatantly wrong. However, neither trial judge nor prosecution nor defence had an opportunity to evaluate the 5.25am entry because the police had withheld it.

Secondly (and sensationally), four entries in the logs and incident report flatly contradict the prosecution's account that Nevill Bamber's body was found downstairs in the kitchen and the other four bodies upstairs. An entry in the radio message log (which the police withheld for nearly nineteen years) reads: "0737: one dead male and one dead female in the kitchen". The telephone message log (which police withheld for nearly nineteen years) records: "0738: one dead male and one dead female found on entry" and at 7:40am the incident log (which police withheld for nearly nineteen years) records a message from D/Ins I.R.: "Police entered premises: 1 dead male; 1 dead female" – and we know from their witness statements that by 7.40am the police had not yet gone upstairs and searched the back of the house, where the other bodies were found. Finally, after they eventually searched this part of the house and finished their task, they reported: "House now thoroughly searched by firearms team. Now confirmed a further 3 bodies found".

Almost immediately on entering the farmhouse, two bodies had been found downstairs in the kitchen. Later, three more bodies had been found upstairs. But most empathically, this is not what the prosecution heard at the trial.

The defence believed that they probably know what happened. The body of Sheila Caffell, which police found upstairs, had first been seen downstairs, in the kitchen.

Dead bodies do not move.

The proposition that Sheila was still alive when police thought she was dead in the kitchen might be dismissed as fanciful if there was not supporting photographic evidence which was not disclosed until 2001. Unfortunately, Bamber's previous defence did not recognize its significance before his 2002 appeal.

Before the trial in 1986, Bamber's defence had access to a large bundle of scene of crime photographs. These included photographs of the dead bodies. In the cases of Nevill and June Bamber rigor mortis, skin discolouration and congealed blood were clearly in evidence. Defence wrongly assumed that these were all the photographs which had been taken. Before the 2002 appeal, however, they were shown another, smaller bundle of 80 – 100 photographs which has previously been withheld.

At Bamber's trial, the prosecution had argued that if Sheila had committed the murders and then killed herself, she would have trodden in blood as she moved about the house but no trace of blood had been found on her feet. No photographic evidence was produced in support. Curiously, the first main bundle of photographs contained no pictures of Sheila's feet. Not so with the withheld second bundle: photographs which had not been available to the Court clearly show blood on her feet.

The withheld second bundle contains even more dramatic evidence. There are several photographs of Sheila. There are no signs of rigor mortis. Her skin is not discoloured. Uncongealed blood flows from her wounds.

Bamber's defence have shown these photographs to leading pathologists. Independently, the pathologists have concluded that Sheila could not have died much mort than an hour and a half before the photographs were taken.

The police photographer did not arrive until shortly after 9am. According to the pathologists, Sheila therefore dies about the time the police entered White House Farm. If so, Bamber did not murder her.

The points which I have made (and there are many others I could make, if we had more time) give rise to grave concern about Bamber's conviction. Their common theme is the non-disclosure of evidence by the police. Nearly sixteen years after the White House Farm murders, the defence first saw the second bundle of photographs. After nearly nineteen years, they discovered that there were radio and telephone logs and an incident report, none of which they had known of previously. It is the understatement of all understatements to say that this is deeply worrying.

Even worse, it is still happening.

Bamber's defence has repeatedly asked for access to:

1. the notebooks and other papers of Inspector Jones who headed the initial investigation and firmly believe Bamber's innocence;
2. the findings of the coroner who inquired into Inspector Jones' sudden death; these have never been made public;
3. the audio recordings of all telephone and radio messages from White House Farm;
4. the audio recordings describing the scene of crime;
5. The video recordings of the scene of crime; and the original radio and telephone messages and incident report.

All these are still being withheld from the defence. On every occasion which the defence has asked for them, Essex Constabulary has refused to provide. I put it directly to the minister and ask her to respond: this is intolerable.

In December, I tabled a Written Parliamentary Question, asking the Home Secretary to instruct the Essex Constabulary to give Mr. Bamber's solicitors all audio tapes relating to events at White House Farm. The Minister replied: "The disclosure of information held by Essex Constabulary is a matter for the Chief Officer of the force". Unfortunately, the Chief Constable has made his position clear; he will not co-operate. One wonders why.

The Minister also stated in her reply: "If the information requested is available under the access provisions of the Data Protection Act 1998 or the Freedom of Information Act then Mr. Bamber may have his own rights to gain access to such information under this legislation". These possible 'rights' have been explored. They do not appear to exist.

It is now time for the Home Office to take matters seriously and look very closely not only at the few points which I have made but also at the whole case which Bamber's defence is presenting. If the Home Office does not do so, it will be perpetuating what a growing number of people believe is one of the greatest miscarriages of justice of out time.
They show that rigor mortis had set in on all victims except Sheila, he says. He is confident the new evidence will lead to a successful third appeal. He said: "My lawyer has the photos. They are absolutely clear – it is quite hard for me to say – there is no question you can see mum and dad have been dead quite some time."

"Sheila still looks pink and while the blood on them is dry, Sheila sis still bleeding".

"Sheila must also have walked on the blood stains on the carpet as in the photos you can clearly see the stains on her feet, even though they said her hands and feet were clean".

Bamber is also excited that his lawyers have recently obtained logs completed by a radio and telephone operator at Essex police headquarters in Springfield.
They wrote down what they were told by the first officers to arrive at the farmhouse, because it was not until 1997 that conversations were tape-recorded.

He said: "The freshest of fresh evidence we have is probably the other scenes of crime logs and the logs taken and written down at the scene and at head office, which confirm what was not disclosed in the written log".

These logs show that police officers had seen somebody moving at an upstairs window, while Bamber was outside with them.

Bamber said: "I don't want to lose focus on the main issues though, such as the non disclosure of the evidence log. If we'd had the radio log we'd have had an alibi for me"

He still hasn't ruled out the possibility that his did Sheila did the killings.

He said: "The evidence appears to be very strong that she did, but we can't rule out that there may have been a third party who we don't know and it's not for me to suggest who it may have been".

Clearly optimistic about the possibility of release, he said, "We were very lucky to get this fresh evidence. As soon as I got it I knew, this is absolute dynamite. I thought 'this is just amazing'".

"It is hard, solid evidence that as soon as it gets before Court it will absolutely win. It has to win."

"we are currently just waiting for someone to make a decision to get my case into Court, waiting for someone to say 'yes', this evidence is so significant we must get this to Court as soon as possible".

"What we have come up with this time is a whole new angle. I have got an alibi and always have had an alibi - this is clear in this new evidence. It can't have been me, it wasn't me and the evidence is there to prove it".

Bamber, now 44, spoke freely and was in a buoyant mood.

The Radio and Telephone Logs
LATEST: Statements from Communications Officer

Also read: The Wireless Message Log and The Editing of the Police Logs

Radio and telephone logs are documents which are written up by a communications officer in order to create an accurate contemporaneous account of the information given over the police radio or the telephone to police headquarters during an incident.

On 7th August 1985 Malcolm Bonnett was on duty in the information room at police headquarters (Chelmsford) and it was his job to make accurate timed recordings of all the radio and telephone messages relayed to him regarding the incident at White House Farm. As an additional safeguard, to ensure he recorded information accurately, Essex police made audio tape recordings of all his radio and telephone conversations.
Bonnett's statement dated 8th November 1985 confirm that it was standard practice to make these audio tape recordings: "As a matter of course all radio and telephone messages are recorded on audio tape as an accurate means of recording."

In March 2004 Essex police complied with a Court Order to hand over the complete radio and telephone logs to Jeremy Bamber's defence lawyers, who were sent document consisting of twenty four pages. Prior to this disclosure the defence had only known about two pages of information, which had been disclosed to the defence in 2001, prior to the last appeal in 2002. Initially the police had only given a single piece of paper to the defence prior to the trial in 1986. This was exhibited at the trial as item 29, the telephone call record of Jeremy Bamber reporting to the police details of a call he had received from his father. But what was not known at the trial was that on the back of this telephone log was the rewritten, edited version of the first page of the radio log. Because the radio log did not form part of the prosecution case at trial, there was no reason for a photocopy of the reverse side to me made and given to the defence. Nor was there a reason for the defence to examine the original telephone log because there was no dispute over the content or the clarity of the photocopy provided to them.

Documents exhibited at trial in bundles given to the defence, the prosecution and the judge are always photocopies. There are only two reasons why the defence may request sight of the original documents, when either the copies are illegible of if they suspect that there had been an addition or deletion to a document. So had the defence looked at the original telephone log in Court and seen the hand written radio message on the back of it, they might have made further enquiries. However at trial, no one looked at the original radio message therefore no one considered why only a single page of radio messages seemed to exist, of why they were not written on the proper form.

Essex police have so far refused to hand over the audio recordings which Malcolm Bonnett states were made of all the radio and telephone messages covering the White house Farm incident on 7th August 1985.

In January 2005, Andrew Hunter MP received a reply to a written parliamentary question to the Home Secretary regarding the failure of the police to hand over copies of these audio recordings. The Home Office Minister stated that the correct way to obtain these recordings would be by written application, under the Freedom of Information Act, to the police. There on 7th February 2005 an official request was made to Essex police to hand over all the relevant audio tape recordings. To date there has been no response.

Obtaining thee audio recordings will serve two purposes:

Firstly, it is the simplest method of proving that the police rewrote and edited the original radio message log to conceal Jeremy Bamber's alibi evidence given by the police at the scene. But even without the audio tapes it can be proved absolutely that the first two pages were edited and rewritten.

Secondly, Essex police are now saying that entries which appear on the radio and telephone logs were a misrepresentation of the facts. They say that Malcolm Bonnet was professionally incompetent in his job and that most of what he wrote down was wrong. Of course Essex police have to criticise Malcolm Bonnett because if his records are accurate, the case against Jeremy Bamber collapses. But even without the audio records the accuracy of Malcolm Bonnett's log keeping can be verified by cross reference to numerous other documents, proving that Essex police do not want the truth to be revealed.

There is clear evidence that the radio and telephone logs were not disclosed to the defence at trial, a fact confirmed by Jeremy Bamber's trial defence lawyers, Judge Rivlin QC (as he now is) and Mr. Lawson, QC. Furthermore these logs were not shown to the prosecution's trial lawyers, Mr. Arlidge QC and his junior Mr. Munday, nor were they shown to the trial judge, Sir Maurice Drake. All of them have confirmed this in writing.

The result of this non disclosure by the police was that Jeremy Bamber received an unfair trial. To establish the fairness of the trial, the Appeal Court states that the defence must meet four strict tests:

> Whether he evidence appears to the Court capable of belief.
> This test has to do with the authenticity of the evidence; in this case, are the radio and telephone logs actual photocopies of genuine documents? Of course the answer is yes so the first test has been passed.
>
> Whether it appears to the Court that the evidence may afford any ground for allowing an appeal.
> This test is about the impact of the new evidence on the safety of the conviction. The non-disclosure of the radio and telephone logs gives rise to two distinct grounds of appeal:

First of all that key documentary evidence has been edited and rewritten in order to hide alibi evidence from the Court and the defence.

Secondly, that non-disclosure of the rest of the radio and telephone logs has led to the Courts being wholly misled over the truthfulness of the prosecution's case. For example, it is now known that at 5.25am Essex police were in conversation with a person inside the house. It is also known that the police originally identified a second baby in the kitchen. Furthermore, we know that DCI Harris used the kitchen telephone to call Dep. Chief Constable Simpson prior to the scenes of crime photographs being taken and that in 2002 the Appeal Court was wholly misled about this issue.

The editing and rewriting of evidence to conceal an alibi would be grounds for allowing an appeal. The misrepresentation of the scenes of crime evidence to the defence and prosecution by concealing documents from them would also be grounds for allowing an appeal.

So, on two separate accounts, test two is satisfied.

c. Whether the evidence which is the subject of the appeal would have been admissible in the proceedings from which the appeal ensures.

This simply means would it have been legal, had it been known about, to use the non disclosure evidence at trial.

This test is met because clearly the radio and telephone logs could have been used had they been available to the defence or prosecution at trial.

d. Whether there is reasonable explanation for the failure to adduce the evidence in those proceedings.

This is what is known as the due diligence test. The Appeal Court requires the defence to establish that it made every reasonable effort prior to the original trial to discover the evidence now being relied on. Could this evidence have been uncovered during the usual enquiries that defence lawyers make prior to trial? Essex police will maintain that they allowed Jeremy Bamber's lawyers free access to all the evidence in this case. To establish this they state that Edmund Lawson QC was shown into an office and told that he could look at all the documents in the case stacked in boxes in that room. But there is no proof that any of those boxes contained the radio and telephone logs, because if they had been there, it is inconceivable that Edmund Lawson QC would not have spotted their significance and asked for copies to be made. Disclosure has not been met. Important documents such as these logs should have been sent to the defence lawyers by the police as a matter of course. We know that these logs were being concealed by the police because they did not even show them to their own lawyers. Nor were they disclosed to the City of London police during their enquiry into the case, nor to the Criminal Cases Review Committee, the defence or the Appeal Court in 2002. In fact, right up to the year 2004, Essex police stated that the radio logs consisted of a single page document written on both sides of the page. Then in March 2004, Essex police were forced to admit that in fact, the radio and telephone logs consisted of twenty four pages – thus they were finally disclosed after having been kept secret in the Chief Constable's safe since 1985.

So the fourth test in met because neither the prosecution nor the defence lawyers of the trial judge knew these logs existed. No one apart from the police knew and no one was ever meant to know that the radio and telephone logs consisted of twenty four pages, because once revealed, the prosecutor's case becomes unsustainable. There was no chance that Jeremy Bamber's lawyers could have discovered the radio and telephone logs for use at his trial in 1986.

Since all four tests laid down by the Appeal Court for adducing fresh evidence have been met in full, it is now simply a matter of time waiting for this evidence to be heard in Court and for the appeal judges to rule upon it.

R. v JEREMY NEVILL BAMBER

In drafting these further submissions, we have taken into consideration in a case of this nature and reminded the Applicant that the fact that the Commission does not exist to provide a further appeal from a decision of the Court of Appeal. Its function is to consider issued which were not apparent at the time of the trial and the appeal, such as new evidence which has come to light since the proceedings were concluded or material which has somehow been ignored or overlooked. If the Commission considers that there is a possibility that a miscarriage of justice has occurred, it is duty bound to refer the case back to the Court of Appeal Criminal Division for a further hearing by that Court on both conviction and sentence.

THE LAW

The terms of reference of the Commission are set out in the Criminal Appeal Act 1995 section 13, which provides as follows:-

(i) 1. A reference of a conviction, verdict, finding or sentence shall not be made under Sections 9 to 12, unless:-
(ii) (a) The Commission considers that there is a real possibility that the conviction, verdict, finding or sentence would not be upheld were the reference to be made.
(iii) (b) The Commission so consider:-

It follows that within the Trial and the Trial Judge having stated there was no other solution to the murders other than "either/or" and confirmed "it has not been argued otherwise" it is clear that neither Defence Counsel Mr.. Rivlin QC or Prosecuting Counsel Mr.. Arlidge QC never had sight of the Radio Logs of the Major Incident Report and this is indeed confirmed by a letter dated 3 March 2004 from the Essex police force solicitor who is only able to "presume" the Radio Logs were made available to Glaysers Solicitors in 2002 and by a letter dated 27 February 2004 from Glaysers Solicitors who confirm the approximate date and circumstances of when the Radio Log was made available at West Hendon Police Station.

It is to the credit of the Essex police force solicitor who, in the letter of 3 March 2004, discloses a further 18 pages of Radio Log and confirms authenticity of the Radio Log with the entry at *"05.25 Firearms team are in <u>conversation</u> with a person inside the farm."*

It was common ground that this Applicant at that time was indeed with the police outside the farmhouse. If indeed the firearms were in "conversation" with a person from inside the house and, if according to the Major Incident Report, an unidentified male was seen at White House Farm, these two documents make compelling testimony to a "third way".

It is submitted, notwithstanding that those filing these submissions have not spoken to either Mr. Arlidge QC or Mr. Rivlin QC or indeed Mr. Justice Drake (who gave a television interview after his retirement from the High Court Bench on this very case) it was considered that no English Counsel would have deliberately been aware of these documents and covertly hidden them from the Defence and as such there was no necessity to interview any of the dramatis personae from the Trial. The said exculpatory documents were simply not made available to the Court per se. It follows that as a consequence Mr. Justice Drake Continues his direction to the Jury in the following manner:

"...and therefore it follows that if you are sure that Sheila did not carry out the killings, it also follows that you must be sure that the defendant did so, and equally, if you are not sure that Sheila did or did not carry out the killings, if you are either sure she did or are uncertain whether she did or not, ten it follows that you have not been made sure that the defence did so, and therefore he would not be guilty, so either way, that second issue I suggest to you are you sure that Sheila did not carry out the killings will lead you to a verdict in this case" (Page 8 A – B) Summing Up

Mr. Justice Drake did however, accentuate upon the responsibilities of the Prosecution and to his full credit as a Trial Judge gave the following warning which would be an indication, never heeded, for the following 20 years of this whole, unsafe and unsound conviction:

"They do, however, have a very stringent obligation which is recognized in our criminal procedure. They have two duties which they have

to perform and which in practice are zealously carried out. First, if in any of those statements there is something that would have been of assistance to the Defendant who is on trial, then it is <u>the duty of the Prosecution on make known that fact to the defence</u>, because under our system of law, the Prosecution do not seek at all costs to secure a conviction. The duty of the Prosecution is to see that justice is done, and if they come across a witness who clearly would be of assistance to the Defence from something he had stated, they are under an obligation to make that fact known to the Defence and they do so." (Page 37 A – C) Summing Up

The failure to disclose to the Defence the Radio Log, now very kindly disclosed by the Essex Police solicitor in the proper format, and the discovery in papers at West Hendon Police of the Major Incident Report, at **the time of trial** was fatal to the Defence and whilst at that time The Human Rights Act was not enacted as legislation, a conviction founded upon a grave violation of a human right within the current legislation can never be deemed safe and must carry the label of "unsound, unsafe and wholly unsatisfactory".

It is evidently clear the Learned Trial Judge, Mr.. Justice Drake, was of the clear opinion and view that all has indeed been disclosed by the Prosecuting Authorities. The Learned Trial Judge admonishes Defence Counsel in the following manner:

"Another matter which I must also refer to that cropped up in Mr. Rivlin's closing speech, is one in which he did expressly make a complaint about the Prosecution handling of the case and a suggestion that the defence had somehow been put at a disadvantage by the Prosecution & ……… Now I must tell you quite bluntly and straight, that he was wrong to make that criticism..." (Page 36 E – F) Summing Up

At all material times it is submitted that both Defence Counsel and Prosecuting Counsel and Mr. Justice Drake were never availed by the Prosecuting Authorities, for reasons that are irrelevant for the purposes of these submissions, to the said documents which clearly call for a case to be argued as "the third way".

SHORT FACTS OF THE CASE

The history of the matter is best set out by para 1 - 2 of the Judgment dated 12 December 2002:

"On 28th October 1986 Jeremy Bamber was convicted of 5 counts of murder by a majority of 10 – 2 following a 19 day trial in the Crown Court at Chelmsford before Drake J and a jury. He was sentenced to life imprisonment with a recommendation that he serve a minimum of 25 years. Following his trial he sought leave to appeal against conviction. His full application as refused on the papers by the single judge but was renewed to the full court. On 20 March 1989 the full court presided over the Lord Chief Justice, Lord Lane, heard his renewed appeal for leave. The court dismissed his application."

The matter proceeded upon the following short and brief facts surrounding what was, is and remains a high profile case requiring the Court of Appeal, Criminal Division extra attention both at the time of the first appeal and subsequent and as evidence by the careful reasoned judgment behind the refusal and what was the careful attention of the Lord Chief Justice Lord Lane. The facts summarized as follows by Justice Lord Kay and no issue is taken by those making these submissions:

"The killings occurred in the early hours of 7th August 1985. All five of those who died met their deaths from gunshot wounds. They were the appellants parents, Ralph Nevill Bamber and June Bamber, his sister, Sheila Caffell, and his sister's 6 year old twins Nicholas and Daniel Caffell. There was no dispute at the trial that four of the five had been murdered. In respect of the fifth, Sheila Caffell, there was an issue, which lay at the very heart of the case, as to whether she had been murdered as the prosecution alleged or whether she had taken her own life as the defence contended."

It is important for the purpose of this application that both (1) The Trial Judge Mr. Justice Drake, (2) Lord Chief Justice Lane at the first appeal and (3) The Court of Appeal, Criminal Division sitting in December 2002 as well as both (a) Prosecuting Counsel at Trial and subsequent Appeals and (b) Defence Counsel at Trial and subsequent Appeals found the following common ground as a basis for a Prosecution / Defence and is accentuated by Lord Justice Kay in the Court's Judgment in December 2002:

"**Unusually in a case of this kind,** it was accepted at trial that there were only **two possible explanations** for the dreadful events of that night. The first, alleged by the prosecution was that the appellant had killed all five members of his family, shooting them with a .22 rifle with the probable motive of inheriting the whole of the family estate. The second, the defence case, was that Sheila Caffell, who had a history of mental illness, had murdered her parents and her two sons with the rifle, and then turned the gun upon herself in an act of suicide. **The view realistically by all at trial was that the facts were common ground enabled <u>any other possibility to be rules out.</u>**"

The Applicant both at Trial and both Appeal Hearings face the prejudicial situation that the Court rather as a matter of law to carry the onus and burden of proof upon the Application having murdered his family, the crown has simply to prove that Sheila Caffell was not the killer and as a consequence the jury were left with "no third way" alternative. Rather then than having to prove the Application guilty the Court concentrated on proving that Sheila Caffell was innocent thus, as a result of "any other possibility being ruled out" would face the jury to convict notwithstanding that the jury convicted by majority decision as opposed to unanimous.

The Court of Appeal, Criminal Division have made clear what, in accordance with these submissions vitiated any possibility of the Applicant having ever received a fair trial by stating that the common ground of "either Bamber or his sister and no other way" was **"unusual in a case of his nature".**

"THE THIRD WAY" SUBMISSON FOR REFERRAL

Submissions made to the Court of Appeal, Criminal Division in December 2002, and at Trial and first Appeal resulted in the following information as the foundation for refusing the Applicant the Appeal:

"**The police were first alerted that something out of the ordinary had occurred when they received a telephone call from the appellant. The call was logged at 3.36am but there was evidenced that made clear**

that it must have been at least 10 minutes earlier. The caller was the appeallant and having given his name and address he said:
"You've got to help me. My father has rang me and said "Please come over. Your sister has gone crazy and has got the gun." Then the line went dead."

He went on say that his sister has history of psychiatric illness and he confirmed that there were guns at his father's house, which was White House Farm, Tolleshunt D'Arcy in Essex. The telephonist contacted the Police Information Room and a police car was dispatched to the father's address. The appellant was asked to meet the police there.

When the police attended at the farm, they were joined by the appellant. There was no sound from the farm save for the barking of a dog and fearing they may be in a hostage situation, the police decided to wait until daylight. At about 7.45am, armed officers entered the farm and found all five occupants dead from gunshot wounds. Mr.. Bamber lay dead in the kitchen, his wife dead on the floor in her bedroom the boys were dead in their bed and Sheila Caffell was lying on the floor of the same room as her mother. Across her chest and pointing at her neck, through which the wounds that had killed her had been fired, was the rifle used to shoot all five members of the family. Beside her body lay a bible. The scene certainly gave the impression that she had shot herself, and the likelihood that this was the case was reinforced by information give to police by the appellant."

The police investigation is summarised as follows and the further basis for upholding the conviction:

"A police enquiry into the matter was at once initiated and it is clear that the senior police officers involved, and to some extent the pathologist who attended, readily accepted at that stage that they were dealing with five deaths for which Sheila Caffell was responsible. However there seem to have been some junior officer, who from an early stage believed everything did not add up. This view was soon echoed by a number of members of the wider family. It was not though until early

September that the real possibility that someone else might have called all five was properly addressed and there was a change in the senior investigating officer. The appellant's ex-girlfriend came forward and gave information to the police. This cause the focus of attention to move to the appellant and another said to be connected with him. Further enquiries were made and as a result the appellant was charged with the five murders"

The representations made to the Court of Appeal, Criminal Division up to para 32 of the said Judgment accounted for occurrences between 03.26am on the day of the incident to the moment police entered the farmhouse.

It was however, missing vital information and documents that the Crown had not disclosed to the Defence at the Trial before Mr.. Justice Drake, at the firs Appeal but which it is conceded may have been placed within the multitude of documents disclosed some 18 years post trial and prior to the Hearings in December 2002 before the Court of Appeal, Criminal Division.

The said documents undermine what was the basis for a conviction "if it was not Sheila Caffell it must have been the Applicant because it provides a third alternative.

THE DOCUMENTS PROVIDING SUBSTANCE FOR A THRID ALTERNATIVE

1. (1) MAJOR INCIDENT REPORT: - item 1 at 03.45 S11 Myall (police officer who attended scene with Applicant logs following) *"UNIDENT MALE"* at *"White House Farm"*. It is important to note that PC Myall is noting at 03.45 an unidentified male at White House Farm when the Applicant was clearly in his company.
2. (2) WIRELESS MESSAGE LOG:- penultimate items reading as follows: *"05.25 Firearms team are in conversation with a person from inside the farm"*

There is further a failure on the part f the Crown to disclose the evidence of PC Mercer who that fateful evening was the dog handler and whose Alsatian dog was specially trained to "sniff" or explosives, firearms or signs from any person who had recently handled a firearm. The dog did indeed approach the Applicant and carry out his trained role without a positive result. Whilst per se this evidence would not necessarily in itself be sufficient to question a conviction it is indeed a strong inference, if it had been made available to the jury, that the Applicant had not recently handled a firearm and as such could no have been responsible for the killings which were carried out by firearm.

There is further evidence of a certain Steven Brian Smith of 23 Tollesbury Road, Tolleshunt D'Arcy; Essex who heard "gunshot sounds" at a time when it was indeed conceded and common ground the Applicant was not at the farm.

There is further all the witness statement and evidence of the senior police officer Taff Jones (who died in somewhat strange and mysterious circumstances) just prior to the trial and his notebooks. All could and should have been properly disclosed especially as he was the Officer who was in charge of the investigation and who did not believe the Applicant committed the said murders, invariable as he would have seen the radio logs (not disclosed) and the major incident report (not disclosed) spoken to PC Mercer and the result of the firearm test carried out by the Alsatian (negative) together with his own observations (no disclosed).

It is submitted thus that there was indeed a third alternative but that the substance to such was simply not disclosed so it became indeed **"unusually common ground"** that either the Applicant killed his family of they were killed by Sheila Caffell.

The Defence never had the opportunity at raising this potential defence. The evidence is quite powerful and overwhelming. At 03.45am PC Myall logged an unidentified male at White House Farm. No further information is given. Had this log been disclosed any Defence Counsel would have made further enquiries with question of the officer. Why a male? What did PC Myall see to make him include such in his log? At 05.25am the Firearms team "in conversation with a person from inside the house" This is indeed perhaps the most powerful evidence that either (a) the real perpetrator was inside the house still or (b) someone in the family was till alive. Any such hypotheses would be exculpatory evidence on the Applicant and should have been disclosed.

DID THE APPLICANT RECEIVE A FAIR TRIAL?

The House of Lords declared in *R v Horseferry Road Magistrates' Court, Ex p Bennett* [1994] 1 AC 42, 68, and recently repeated in *Attorney General's Reference (No 2 of 2001)* [2003] UKHL 68, [2004] 2 WLR 1, para 13, it is "axiomatic" **"that a person charged with having committed a criminal offence should receive a fair trial and that, if he cannot be tried fairly for that offence, he should not be tried for it at all".** Article 6 of the European Convention required that the trial process, viewed as a whole, must be fair. Any answer given to the questions raised by these appeals must be governed by that cardinal and overriding requirement.

While the focus of Article 6 of the Convention is on the right of a criminal defendant to a fair trial, it is a right to be exercised within the framework of the administration of the criminal law: as Lord Steyn pointed out in *Attorney General's Reference (No 3 of 1999)* [2001] 2 AC 91, 118,

> **"The purpose of the criminal law is to permit everyone to go about their daily lives without fear of harm or person or property. And it is in the interests of everyone that serious crime should be effectively investigated and prosecuted. There must be fairness to all sides. In a criminal case this required the court to consider triangulation of interests. It involves taking into account the position of the accused, the victim and his or her family, and the public".**

The European Court had repeatedly recognized that individual rights should not be treated as if enjoyed in a vacuum: *Sporrong and Lonnroth v Sweden* (1982) 5 EHRR 35, 52, para 69: *Sheffield and Horsham v United Kingdom* (1998) 27 EHRR 163, 191, para 52. As lord Hope of Craighead pointed out in *Montgomery v HM Advocate* [2003] 1 AC 641, 673:

> "The rule of law lies at the heart of the Convention. It is not the purpose of article 6 to make it impracticable to bring those who are accused of crime to justice. The approach which the Srasbourg court has taken to the question whether there are sufficient safeguards recognises this fact."

The institutions and procedures established to ensure that a criminal trial is fair vary almost infinitely from one jurisdiction to another, the product of historical, cultural and legal tradition. Instead, the achievement of fairness in a trial or indictment tests above all on the correct and conscientious performance of their roles by judge, prosecuting counsel, defending counsel and jury. Saved in defined circumstances (such as when ruling on the voluntariness of a confession in a voir dire or, much more rarely, a specific allegation of official misconduct) the judge is not a factual decision-maker. His task is to ensure that the trial is conducted in a fair and even-handed way. For this latter purpose he is entrusted with numerous discretions (see Rosemary

Pattenden, *Judicial Discretion and Criminal Litigation,* 2nded 1990). The duty of prosecuting counsel, recently considered by the Judicial Committee of the Privy Council in *Randall v The Queen* [2002] UKPC 19, [2002] 1 WLR 2237, para 10, is not to obtain a conviction at all costs but to act as a minister of justice. As Rand J put it in the Supreme Court of Canada in *Boucher v The Queen* [1955] SCR 16, 24-25:

"Counsel have a duty to see that all available legal proof of the facts is presented: it should be done fairly and pressed to its legitimate strength but it must also be done fairly."

Defending counsel are also subject to clear professional rules: they may, in fact must, not invent a case for their client or pursue serious accusations in the absence of material to support them: Code of Conduct for the Bar of England and Wales, paragraph 708 (e).

It is submitted that this Applicant, by the clear absence and availability of the Documents capable of being argued by Defence Counsel as exculpatory, defined the trial as being clearly unfair with the Defence seriously disadvantaged.

DISCLOSURE

At the time of the trial there was a duty to disclose material information subject to certain exceptions which are contained in the Attorney General's Guidelines (Disclosure of Information to the Defence Cases to be tried on Indictment) laid down in 1981 (74 Cr.App.R 302). Amongst the exceptions for example were cases were a statement disclosed the identity of an informant or there were reasons for fearing that disclosure of identity would put a family in danger. There can be no doubt in this case that there were no such fears that disclosure of the radio log and major incident report, evidence from the police dog handler, evidence from a deceased officer would place anyone in danger. In those days the decision perforce, had to be made without reference to the Court. There was no provision for the Crown to have ex parte access to the trial judge and if sought it would almost certainly have been refused. If an application had been granted it would almost certainly have been viewed as a material irregularity.

It is also without question a serious violation of the bar Counsel's Code of Conduct if Counsel is aware of exculpatory material not placing such before the Court if not the defence.

Fairness ordinarily requires that any material held by the prosecution which weakens its case or strengthens that of the defendant, if not relied on as part of its formal case against the defendant, should be disclosed to the defence. Bitter experience shows that miscarriages of justice occur where such material is withheld from disclosure. The golden rule is that full disclosure of such material should be made.

Until December 1981, the prosecution duty was to make available, to the defence, witnesses whom the prosecution did not intend to call, and earlier inconsistent statements of witnesses whom the prosecution were to call: See Archbold, *Pleading, Evidence and Practice in Criminal Cases*, 41st ed (1982) ([1982] 1 All ER 734) extended the prosecution's duty of disclosure somewhat, but laid down no test other than one of relevance ("has some bearing on the offence(s) charged and the surrounding circumstance of the case") and left the decision on disclosure to the judgment of the prosecution and prosecuting counsel.

In *R v Ward* [1993] 1 WLR 619, 674 this limited approach to disclosure was held to be inadequate:

An incident of a defendant's right to a fair trial is a right to timely disclosure by the prosecution of all material matters which affect the scientific case relied on by the prosecution, that is, whether such matters strengthen or weaken the prosecution case or assist the defence case. This duty exists whether or no specific request for disclosure of details of scientific evidence is made by the defence. Moreover, this duty is continuous: it applies not only in the pre trial period but also throughout the trial".

The rule stated with reference to scientific evidence, because that is what the case concerned, but the authority was understood to be laying down a general test based on relevance: see *R v Keane* [1994] 1 WLR 746, 752.

The problem reconciling an individual defendant's right to a fair trial with secrecy as is necessary in a democratic society in the interests of national security or the prevention or investigation of crime is inevitably difficult to resolve in a liberal society governed by the rule of law. Complaints of violation have been made against member states including the United Kingdom, some of what have exposed flaws in or malfunctioning of UK domestic procedures. The European Court has however long accepted that some operations must be conducted secretly if they are to be conducted effectively: *Klass v Federal Republic of Germany* (1978) 2 EHRR 214, 232, paragraph 48.

In *Edwards v United Kingdom* (1992) 15 EHRR 417 there was a prosecution failure to disclose relevant information, but no PII issued had been raised. The omission was held to have been rectified by the appeal process. The applicant in *Bendenoun v France* (1994) 18 EHRR 54 similarly complained of non disclosure by the prosecution: his application failed because (paragraph 52) the undisclosed material had not been relied on by the prosecution and he had given no sufficiently specific reasons for requesting the material in question.

Chahal v United Kingdom (1996) 23 EHRR 413 arose from protracted immigration proceedings and did not involve a complaint under article 6. But the case has proved very influential, since in it the Court held (paragraph 144) that the expedient of appointing security-cleared counsel, instructed by the Court, who would cross examine the witnesses and generally assist the Court to test the strength of the State's case, served to illustrate (paragraph 131):

"that there are techniques which can be employed which both accommodate legitimate security concerns about the nature and sources of intelligence information and yet accord the individual a substantial measure of procedural justice".

Rowe and Davis v United Kingdom (2000) 30 EHRR 1 arose from the proceedings in which an important ruling had been given by the Court of Appeal in England (paragraph 20 above). Having reviewed the facts of the case and the development of English practice, the Court found that the applicants' rights under article 6 had been violated. In doing so, the Court recognised it (paragraph 60) as a

> **"fundamental aspect of the right to a fair trial that criminal proceedings, including the elements of such proceedings which relate to procedure, should be adversarial and that there should be equality of arms between the prosecution and defence. The right to an adversarial trial means, in a criminal case, that both prosecution and defence must be given the opportunity to have knowledge of and comment on the observations filed and the evidence adduced by the other party. In addition Article 6 (1) requires, as indeed does English law, that the prosecution authorities should disclose to the defence all material evidence in their possession for or against the accused".**

This has been the domestic law under the Attorney General's 1981 Guidelines, but has ceased to be so in 1996. The Court continued:

"However, as the applicants recognised, the entitlement to disclosure of relevant evidence, is not an absolute right. In any criminal proceedings there may be competing interests, such as national security or the need to protect witnesses at risk of reprisals or keep secret police methods of investigation of crime, which must be weighed against the rights of the accused. In some cases it may be necessary to withhold certain evidence from the defence so as to preserve the fundamental rights of another individual or to safeguard an important public interest. However, only such measures restricting the rights of defence which are strictly necessary are permissible under Article 6(1). Moreover, in order to ensure that the accused receives a fair trial, any difficulties caused to the defence by a limitation on its rights must be sufficiently counterbalance by the procedures followed by the judicial authorities. In cases where evidence has been withheld from the defence on public interest grounds, it is not the role of this Court to decide whether or not such non disclosure was strictly necessary since, as a general rule, it is for the national courts to assess the evidence before them. Instead, the European Court's task is to ascertain whether the decision making procedure applied in each case complied, as far as possible, with the requirements of adversarial proceedings and equality of arms and incorporated adequate safeguards to protect the interests of the accused"

In *PG and JH v United Kingdom* (4 September 2001, unreported, appn no 44787/98) the prosecution had sought to withhold in public interest grounds certain information relating to the installation of a listening device. A police officer declined to answer questions put to him in cross examination by defence counsel because his answers might reveal sensitive material. The judge then, with the consent of the defence, put questions to the officer in the absence of the defendants and their lawyers and concluded that the benefit of the answers to the defence was slight, if any, while the damage to the public interest if the answers were made public would be great. The Judge refused to exclude the same grounds as in *Jasper and Fitt* (paragraph 71) that the withholding of the officer's report and the procedure adopted to examine him had not violated article 6. The Court held (paragraph 71):

> "The Court also notes that the material which was not disclosed in the present case formed no part of the prosecution case whatever, and was never put to jury. The fact that the need for disclosure was at all times under assessment by the trial judge provided a further, important safeguard in that it was his duty to monitor throughout the trial the fairness or otherwise of the evidence being withheld. It has not been suggested that the judge was not independent and impartial within the meaning of Article 6.he was fully verse in all the evidence an issues in the case and a position to monitor the relevance to the defence of the withheld information both before and during the trial".

In both *Atlan v United Kingdom* (2001) 34 EHRR 833 and *Dowsett v United Kingdom* (24 June 2003, unreported, appn no 394829/98) unanimous findings of violation of Article 6(1) were made. In the first of these cases (paragraphs 44-45) the prosecution repeatedly denied the existence of undisclosed material and failed to inform the judge of the true position, when it appeared that there had been undisclosed material directly bearing in the defence advanced at trial. In the second case it was held that the prosecution's failure to disclose material at the trial, although partly cured in the Court of Appeal (paragraph 46) had not been wholly cured (paragraphs 47-49)

It is highly unlikely, in fact submitted as impossible, that Prosecuting Counsel, the trial judge Mr. Justice Drake, Defence Counsel at three Hearings were made aware of the material and failed to disclose such or use such. What is evident however is that the Court of Appeal sitting in December 2002 was also not made aware of such. The inference in such must be that the said documents were inadvertently "buried with myriads of documents" when finally disclosed in 200 and since the basis of the previous CCRC Reference was upon forensic evidence, such exculpatory material in two simple pieces paper which provide a third alternative, were simply not considered.

These submissions lay or apportion no fault upon any party. No do these submissions form the basis of any accusatorial inquisition upon Prosecuting Counsel, Defence Counsel or any Members of the two diverse Court of Appeal justices who presided over the appeals of this Applicant.

The basis of the conviction was common ground that "either Sheila did it and if she did not Bamber did it" was indeed noticed by Lord Justice May and noted as unusual. As stated previously the Court of Appeal is however, not Court of Trial. It is a Court of Review. The Court has not established any precedent for acting on the Court's own motion. The Court is bound by submissions made by Defence and Prosecuting Counsel. The Court is specifically precluded from opening their own investigation into the facts of the case or documents. The Court of Appeal in December 2002 would not have been served all the papers made available to the defence by the CCRC and the main thrust of the argument was focused upon the forensic evidence and the DNA. The "third way" did not attract the appropriate consideration although the comment by Lord Justice Kay as the position being "unusually in a case of this nature" was judicial hindsight and wisdom at its highest.

It was indeed so "unusual" that it was not the case owing to the failure to properly disclose the documents.

A failure to disclose not necessarily be intentive. It may be inadvertent. What is important is the significance had the documents been disclosed, not so much during the appellate hearings, but at trial. As stated previously, those indicted of serious crimes are tried before a jury. There are no trials before the Court of Appeal, Criminal Division. This Applicant was convicted by a majority decision of 10-2 on the basis that if Sheila Caffell did not murder her family then it was the Applicant. No alternatives were proposed albeit such being somewhat in unusual circumstances. The documents subsequently disclosed make a third way not only possible, probable, but open a line of defence which had such been available may well have altered the pendulum in favour of the Defence at Trial.

BASIS OF SUBMISSION FOR REFERRAL

The test is whether the Court of Appeal in hearing the appeal of this Applicant has during the appeal hearings in December 2002 sufficient material before it to properly and fairly evaluate what would have been the inevitable, albeit regrettable, consequences of the failure of the Crown to make certain disclosures to the Defence at Trial. It is submitted that such material would have persuaded the said Court by virtue of its mandatory requirement. It clearly was available at trial in first instance and not disclosed and as such not argued.

CONCLUSION

The test for a referral, it is submitted, is not whether there would be any likelihood of success by virtue of a referral per se. It is whether the Criminal Appeal Act 1995 s.9-12 can be properly applied. We have detailed the basis at the beginning of these submissions. We are of the view that all the facts and circumstances were not made available to the Court of Appeal for them to properly evaluate on the basis outlines and by the failure of the Crown to disclose at trial potentially exculpatory evidence by virtue of the precedent and state necessarily make a fresh application to the Court of Appeal, Criminal Division likely to succeed.

We therefore request this matter be referred to the Court of Appeal on the basis as outlined above and herein confirm our view that exceptional circumstances do arise for the Commission to depart from the constraints levied upon it and treat this matter, by virtue also of its inevitable consequences, as prioritive.

REGINA
V
JEREMY NEVILL BAMBER

"An informal spoken exchange of news and ideas between two or more people"

It follows that by any interpretation at 05.25am, when the Applicant was outside White House Farm in the company of the police; the firearms team where in conversation (informal spoken exchange of news and ideas between two or more people) with a person from inside the farm. There can be no misunderstanding of this vital piece of information either in law, diction or language. Whilst this Applicant was with the police there existed the clearest of evidence that there was someone, a person, inside the farm. It follows the conviction based upon the fact that whilst this Applicant has murdered his entire family prior to attending the farm with police, with the existence of a person in conversation from inside the farm with the police and such evidence not having been made available for trial, the conviction is clearly unsafe and most unsatisfactory.

17 MARCH 2004
R. v Jeremy Nevill Bamber

These further submissions should be in conjunction with the application to the Criminal Cases Review Commission filed on 8th March 2004. In accordance with the instructions received from the Commission dated 10th March 2004 further information is in the form of these submissions. For the purposes of these addendum submissions it is necessary to recite the legislation levied upon any submissions made to the Commission.

THE LAW

The terms of reference of the Commission are set out in the Criminal Appeal Act 1995 section 13, which provides as follows:

(j) 2. A reference to a conviction, verdict, finding or sentence shall not be made under any of Sections 9 to 12, unless: -

(ii) (a) The Commission considers that there is a real possibility that the conviction, verdict, finding or sentence would not be upheld were the reference to be made.

(iii) (b) The Commission so consider: -

2. (j) in the case of a conviction, verdict or finding, **because of an argument or evidence not raised in the proceedings which led to it, or on any appeal, or application for leave to appeal against it,** or

(ii) in the case of a sentence, because of an argument on a point of law or information not so raised, and

(iii) in the case of an appeal against conviction, verdict, finding or sentence had been determined or leave to appeal against it has been refused.

(2) Nothing in Sub Section 1 (b)(i) or (c) would prevent the making of a reference if it appears to the Commission that there are exceptional circumstances which justify making it.

DISCLOSURE

We have already outlines in detail the legal submissions regarding disclosure and it is not necessary to recite such for the purposes of these submissions. We have already stated that disclosure is a matter of law regulated by procedure.

Clearly, the existence of the Radio Logs and Major Incident Report should have been disclosed by the CPS to the Applicant as part of their primary disclosure obligation pursuant to section 3(1)(a) Criminal Procedure and Investigations Act 1996. Any document which might reasonably found an application for a charged to be quashed, and/or to be stayed as amounting to an abuse of the process of the court, is a document which had a potential to **"undermine the case for the prosecution against the accused".** Moreover, failure to disclose to the Applicant the existence of such document, is clearly contrary to the spirit and intendment of the Guidelines issued by Attorney – General (whether pre or post the Criminal Procedure and Investigations Act 1996, i.e. whether once had regard to the Guidelines issued 18th December 1981 or the current Guidelines issued 29t November 2000)

Attached to these addendum submissions is a letter from the Essex police solicitor, Mr. Adam Hunt to Paul Martin & C Solicitors dated 8th March 2004. It is important to note two matters within the said correspondence:

1. (a) "I am unable to confirm whether your client did or did not have disclosed to him the documents referred to as the radio log and Major Investigation Project. I suggest that this work is

unnecessary since your client's legal records, including the disclosure schedules, will confirm the point."

2. (b) "I am unable to comment on what was accepted as common ground at the original trial but it is not, in my opinion, clear that this was common ground at the appeal."

It is evidently clear that Mr.> Hunt is clearly in error on the understanding of the basis of prosecution both at trial and appeal. It was at all material times common ground that this was a case of "either / or" without any basis for a third possibility. The correspondence from Mr. Edmund Lawson QC (then Junior Counsel at Trial) states as follows and is recited in it entirety:

"Slightly belated thanks for this and your supplementary e-mail. I was prompted to respond by the receipt here today – for which thanks – of the hard copy of your submission to the CCRC. My apologies for not responding earlier: usual excuses of distractions caused buy other work etc....

For what it's worth, I've no recall of seeing the radio logs to which you refer. I do recall that we debated for a long time and by reference to all available material whether we could sensibly advance the argument that a third party (i.e. not JB or his sister) could have committed the murders and concluded that we could not Precisely what information / evidence we had before us

THREE times a week at odd times of the day or night a lone figure in plimsolls slips into a private North London cemetery. The grave he goes to is unmarked, except by flowers. It contains the remains of Colin Caffell's twins, Daniel and Nicholas.

The headstone, still missing more than a year after their burial, is being made by their potter father's loving hands.

It will be worked in clay and coated in bronze and quietly place at the head of the grave when the blame has been apportioned and the fuss dies down.

The design and inscription will be based on the last bedtime story the twins heard, their Enid Blyton favourite The Enchanted Wood.

It was read to the six year olds by Jeremy Bamber's girlfriend Julie Mugford just three days before their grisly deaths.

Colin Caffell's pale blue eyes are blank as you ask how he feels about the man who murdered his sons.

"No I don't hate Jeremy, what's the point". Other members of the family have kept themselves going on their hatred."

Happy.

"I've got through it by blocking out the ghastly things that happened and just clinging to the happy memories I have of us all together."

He swallows and is voice is almost a whisper. "I have so many good memories that I don't want to think about what happened that night, I don't want to know."

In the past 33 year old Colin has learned to live with the stigma of being caught up in the massacre of the people he loved most.

He has become numb to the indignity of police prying. But the unofficial trial of his ex wife Sheila - unstable, lonely and sad – still hurts.

News of the killings was broken to him by police on the doorstep when he got back from the laundry that morning in August last year. Colin's handsome, gentle face froze in shock. Later at Jeremy Bamber's house, he cried.

Mind.

He has chosen not to ask for details of how Sheila, Dan and Nicholas died and he has not seen the police pictures of the blood spattered corpses.

But a year later he still can't sleep for wondering what really happened, and whether they knew – or felt – anything.

His mind goes back 11 years to the Three Horseshoes pub in London's Hampstead where he met Sheila. Colin was introduced to the strikingly pretty girl everyone called Bambs.
She was 17 and enrolled at the expensive secretarial school St Godric's. But she only had one ambition – to be a top model.

They became lovers and the following year, when Sheila found herself pregnant, the family tensions that would drive her to breaking point surfaced.

It was Sheila's mother June Bamber who arranged the abortion.

"We half thought about keeping the baby, but Mrs Bamber was furious," said Colin.

"She fixed up the abortion. Bambs was very unhappy and upset. It screwed her up."

Stern.

But a carrot always came with June Bamber's stern religious stick.

So when Sheila had the abortion she was allowed to go to modelling school and live in a little Chelsea flat paid for by her parents.

She developed a growing obsession about her looks. "She needed constant reassurance," said Colin. "She was a very beautiful woman but she needed to be told that all the time."

As Sheila struggled in her career, the bright spot in her life was her relationship with Colin.

"We had no money," he said. "We lived on my grant from art school, but we were desperately in love."

GRUESOME police photographs lie at the heart of Jeremy Bamber's latest bid to overturn his murder conviction.

Taken by scenes of crime photographers, they show the bodies of his adoptive parents, Nevill and June Bamber, and his sister Sheila "Bambi" Caffell, at White House Farm, Tolleshunt D'Arcy, on August 7th 1985.

Bamber believes they will help him show he was wrongfully convicted of murdering the three adults and Sheila's six year old twin boys Daniel and Nicholas.

When the shocking crime was first discovered, police believed Sheila, in a moment of madness, had shot her parents and twins before turning the gun on herself. Bamber had told them she often had mad bouts with his parents.

Now Bamber – who has already lost two appeals – says the police photographs support the initial theory.

> He added: "Up until recently people have had a misconception about what happened. People now say 'well he's been in there 20 years, he must have done it' and it's not like that."

> "I was given a 25 year sentence originally, but that was upped to a whole life term by (then Home Secretary Michael) Howard. Tree years ago that was capped to 25 years again, but it's really up to the parole board when I'm released."

> "I hope the new evidence we have will see me released by the end of the year."

> Looking to the future, a visit to his parent's grave, at the parish church of Tolleshunt D'Arcy, is top of his things to do when he is finally released.

> He said: "I would very much like to do that of course, but it would also be lovely to be with friends"

"The whole point would be to have the choice to do what I would like to do; it would be lovely to do what I choose."

For now, his fate rests in the hands of those holding his appeal, and despite his earlier certainty, Bamber hesitated as he spoke on the outcome:

"I hope they listen, but I still hold some cynicism. I'm just looking forward to the future."

Asked if he really did kill his family, Bamber had only one answer: "No."

Rough Justice.

When the local doctor's wife, Diane Jones got arrested for drink driving in her car, I noticed that her car was parked for a long time in the front garden of a local farmers bungalow which was situated about 50 yards from the main farmhouse. Later Coggeshall became alive with rumours. When Diane Jones disappeared press men and police were everywhere.
3 different local mothers told me quite clearly that they would not look outside Coggeshall for her killer.

Also a local farmer who had domestic problems and was sent to prison for assaulting his wife. Later on he married again. One day I saw the farmer's new wife walking alone and she was crying. I asked if I could help. She said no; please do not let Jimmy see me talking to you. She said he is going to hurt someone that I am fond of; I asked is there no one you can talk to about your worries? She told me that she intended to discuss her problems with another farmer's wife, Mrs Bamber, who was a religious person.

When working in Coggeshall I used to park my bus in a Coggeshall car park. I used to keep racing pigeons so during my lunchtime I could keep my training results up to date. One day I was in my bus when a loud scattering effect happened. I was quite shocked. Parked next to me was a 4x4 land rover – something had come out of this vehicle and hit my bus. When I went to investigate a local farmer was standing in front of the land rover with a .22 rifle with a silencer on the end of the rifle. What the farmer had done was to throw a box of .22 bullets in the range rover. Then I heard the farmer say, next time these bullets come at you they will come from this, he waved his gun frantically. The people in the range rover parked next to me were Mr. and Mrs Bamber who later on were murdered. They used to bank in Coggeshall bank. The local farmer was saying that Mr. Bamber could have helped him when he was sent to prison for assaulting his wife.

I feel this information should have been heard at Jeremy Bamber's murder trial. As I stated early on in this book that I never received a copy of my statement. I often wonder what the reaction would have been if Jeremy Bamber's sister had been found guilty of these dreadful murders?
Jeremy Bamber's conviction for the family murders left more questions than answers. Not only must justice be done, justice should be seen to be done. However, in this case, I feel an unjust view was concluded.

The local doctor's wife Diane Jones vanished after leaving a local pub the Woolpack Inn, in Coggeshall. Also a couple with their children who were staying in a local farmer's bungalow left without a trace. Then later the local farmer used a farm tractor and trailer to clear his bungalow of carpets, curtains and furniture. I feel the police should have searched this bungalow, because something mysterious happened there. Can you imagine some time later when I was told local farmer Jimmy Bell had travelled to Norfolk to find his second wife. He then murdered his lovely wife, God bless her soul, then killed himself. He certainly was disturbed and a very angry person. He also threatened Mr. Bamber, who was later found murdered with his family. I feel the police were very wrong not to connect these killings. I have a great deal of respect for the police. However, mistakes can be made. One Essex police officer said to me personally about the Bamber killings – he said we got it wrong from the very start at the White House Farm scene of the Bamber murders.

One point that I want to stress and mention is that although Dr Jones was questioned and interviewed by Essex police, Dr Jones was never charged with any offence.

So the question still remains. Who then did kill the local doctor's wife Diane Jones?

Dr Jones life was turned upside down with all the enquiries – yet many local residents have a good word for their doctor.

Many more strange events happened to me whilst working in Coggeshall – as I result I bought a tree and a Statue of the Madonna Virgin Mary carved in to a statue, which I gave to St Peter's Church in Coggeshall.

This was to appease the bad vibes that were happening in Coggeshall.

The last time before Jimmy Bell the local farmer spoke to me. He said I did not do it? Later on he kissed his second wife and then killed himself.

Welcome Back

LATEST NEWS

GEORGE GALLOWAY TABLES QUESTION RE BAMBER 1 May 2007

I am pleased to confirm that I have today received a note from George Galloway MP who confirms that he has tabled a question in the House of Commons for the Home Secretary. The questions is as follows: TO THE HOME SECRETARY:- WHAT ARE THE IMPLICATIONS OF THE PASSING OF A POLYGRAPH TEST BY JEREMY BAMBER AND IF THE HOME SECRETARY WILL MAKE A STATEMENT. The reply is due on 14th May 2007! I express my thanks to Mr Galloway for tabling this question in the House. I have uncovered the final piece of evidence that will prove Jeremy Bamber's wrongful conviction and may well result in prosecutions for certain people.

JEREMY PASSED A POLYGRAPH TEST IN PRISON TODAY THE 19TH APRIL 2007

see questions and results

The following is a summary of the evidence collected over the past 4 years which had been previously undisclosed to us and has since been submitted to the Criminal Cases Review Commission asking them to refer this case back to the Court of Appeal.

This evidence was not available at the original trial and it is our wish that the Court of Appeal consider a retrial where this may be presented to a jury in an open court – this we feel would be the correct and fair way to proceed.

The police were in conversation with someone inside the house after Jeremy had been with the police for over an hour and a half

The police did not disclose at trial that they could alibi Jeremy, documents establishing this came to light after the failed appeal in 2002.

An entry in the radio monitoring log states that the police were in conversation with someone from inside the house. This was two hours prior to them entering the premises and some hours after Jeremy had been with him.   Evidence: radio logs

Two police officers and Jeremy had seen someone walk in front of the bedroom window

This verified the fact that two police officers had seen someone walking in front of an upstairs window, confirmed by Jeremy when they were watching the house soon after their arrival. A report of this sighting was sent to headquarters by police radio but has never been disclosed and was later dismissed as 'shadows' – this begs the question of what caused those 'shadows'? All radio messages were logged by hand and recorded on audio tape. The radio logs made available to the court appear to have been edited and rewritten. Access to these audio recordings would reveal the truth of this but Essex police refuse to hand them over for analysis.

The Essex coroner was provided with evidence sufficient for him to allow the release of the bodies for burial and cremation. The police had informed him that the investigation was ongoing but on the basis of four murders and a suicide. The documents and evidence to substantiate this were lost as were the coroner's files and records – where are the duplicate copies? **Freedom Of Information Act Ombudsman still trying to obtain police pocket books from Essex police, so far without success.**

A male and a female body was seen in the kitchen prior to the police entering the house and identified by different police officers after entry was made to the kitchen

Prior to entering the house two police officers looked into the kitchen through the window and identified a female body. On entering the house the raid team discovered a male and a female body in the kitchen and three further bodies upstairs – all were assumed to be deceased.

There was an operator monitoring a telephone which was off the hook in the kitchen. This was also being recorded. As the police entered the kitchen voices and movement could be heard and this was written in the log. The audio recording is being withheld by Essex police. It would reveal what was being said by whom and why. This is important because at 7.30am there was a male and a female body in the kitchen yet when the crime scene photographs were taken later the female body had disappeared from the kitchen and appeared in the main bedroom with just the male being photographed downstairs in the kitchen. Evidence: communication logs and excerpts from statement of APS John Manners

The kitchen telephone was used by Chief Superintendent Harris prior to the crime scene photographs being taken or any forensic examination of the phone

In 2002 the appeal judges were told by the police that the kitchen telephone had not been touched or moved prior to the crime scene photographs being taken. The radio and telephone logs prove that in fact Chief Superintendent Harris used this telephone to contact Deputy Chief Constable Simpson. Thereby destroying fingerprints and other evidence and causing the crime scene photographs to be compromised.

A crime scene video was taken by the police of the inside of the house, dictaphones were also used by investigating officers as they examined the house. The video tape and the audio tapes made that morning are still being withheld by Essex police. **Freedom Of Information Act Ombudsman still trying to obtain this evidence from Essex police, so far without success.**

Sheila's feet can be seen to be blood stained in previously undisclosed photographs

The courts have always been told that Sheila's feet were spotlessly clean. No photographs were available to the jury showing the soles of her feet. The pathologist gave evidence that the soles of her feet were clean yet photographs now available show the soles of her feet revealing them to be blood stained. **Photographic evidence cannot be shown on this site.**

The pathologist wrote in his hand written pathology notes that Sheila's hands were blood stained yet left this out of his witness statement and trial evidence telling the court her hands were clean

The pathologist also told the jury and the court that Sheila's hands were clean and stated this in his witness statement. Why it was edited out that her hands were bloodstained as documented in his hand written autopsy notes in not known.

Evidence: extract from hand written post-mortem notes

No time of death analysis has been disclosed

It has always been standard practice for a pathologist to take a core body temperature and assess the stage of rigor mortis in order to ascertain an approximate time of death – it is common knowledge that procedure is time, place and cause of death yet if indeed these procedures were followed the finding on the time of death have never been made available or given to the court.

Defence wounds on Mr and Mrs Bamber show deep fingernail scratch marks. These can be seen on photographs which were again undisclosed to the jury and yet the pathologist makes no mention of them

Defence wounds on both Mr and Mrs Bamber show fingernail scratch marks made by someone with long fingernails. The crown's pathologist made no mention of these injuries in his autopsy report or trial evidence. It was only when the undisclosed photographs were looked at that these could be clearly seen. Why were Sheila's long fingernails not scraped for samples? Jeremy's hands and fingernails were scrutinised and found to be clean and his fingernails short. **Photographic evidence cannot be shown on this site.**

Sheila's wounds were still bleeding when she was photographed estimating her death to be at least three hours after Jeremy has an accepted alibi, being with the police

Crime scene photographs show that Sheila's wounds were still bleeding at the time of the photographing. This puts her time of death no earlier than 7am, at least three hours after Jeremy has been outside with the police. Evidence: excerpts from statement of PS Ian Maynes also see photo 28/07/05 on

Sheila's body was restaged by the police prior to the taking of the crime scene photographs. The police had

removed the rifle and then replaced it giving a false impression of the crime scene

At the 2002 appeal the crown wanted to introduce evidence that Sheila's body was moved after her death in order to prove she was murdered. What the crown did not inform the court and the defence did not discover until later was that prior to the crime scene photographs being taken Essex police had removed the rifle from her body, standing it against the bedroom window frame. It was photographed in this position prior to it being photographed on her body. This is confirmed by a police officer stationed outside in an unused statement where she states seeing what appeared to be a rifle in the window over an hour before any crime scene photographs were taken.

Later when the photographs were taken of Sheila the rifle was replaced on her body and her hands positioned by police officers who used a bible to prop up one arm in order to keep it in position for the photographs. This gave a wholly false photographic record of the scene. Evidence: extract from COLP interview with PS Adams also statement of WPS J Jeapes

A note consistent with a suicide note recovered by the police along with the bible found on Sheila was kept out of the evidence chain

On studying the crime scene photographs of the bible found open on Sheila's body it can be seen that a highly relevant hand written note is sticking out from between the pages of the bible. The parts which can clearly be read on enlarging the photographs are highly consistent with a suicide note. There is no record of this note. The police have kept it out of the evidence and it has never been disclosed to neither the prosecution nor the defence. **Photographic evidence cannot be shown on this site.**

Essex police told the appeal court that apart from two stools nothing was touched or moved in the kitchen. Photographs taken prove that two kitchen chairs were moved against the kitchen door prior to the crime scene photographs being taken. Only a policeman could have done this

On rechecking photographs of the kitchen it can be seen that chairs have been placed in front of the door the police entered through. At the 2002 appeal the judges thought this confusing and dismissed it as photographic foreshortening. The raid team police swore statements saying they did not move these chairs but how could they have entered the kitchen if the chairs were already there? Examination of enlarged photographs show the chairs were so close to the kitchen door as to make it impossible to gain entry and so they must have been moved after the police came in.

The personal pocket books of all the police officers who entered the house that morning have been applied for but Essex police have refused to make these available to the defence or the Freedom of Information Ombudsman. **Photographic evidence cannot be shown on this site.**

Two sound moderators for the .22 rifle were recovered from the house – not by police but by prosecution witnesses. These were given to the police, one on the 12 th August 1985 and one on the 11 th September 1985

A prosecution witness handed one to the police on the 12 th August 1985 and handed the other one to them on the 11 th September 1985. Both sound moderators were the same make and model. The first one was taken to a forensic laboratory and examined and taken away the same day for finger printing. During this finger printing process the sound moderator was dismantled, examined and photographed. It was given a forensic reference number and exhibit label. Evidence: excerpts from police action reports

Prior to these witnesses handing one of the sound moderators to the police they admit in their statement to using a razor blade to remove what they believe to be a flake of blood from one end and trying to dismantle it Evidence: excerpts from cross examination of Peter Eaton and statement of David Boutflour

Forensic documents, witness statements and police logs were altered to give the impression that only one sound moderator was recovered from White House Farm when in fact two were discovered

After the second sound moderator was given to the police it was given a different exhibit label and submitted to the same forensic laboratory for examination. Some time later it was decided by Essex police to tell the forensic lab both sound moderators were one and the same and could they alter their records to show this. The prosecution witnesses left out of their witness statements and trial evidence that they had submitted two sound moderators to the police and not one as sworn in evidence.

All of the above can be proven and substantiated by reference to previously un disclosed crime scene logs, photographs, witness statements, radio and telephone logs and pocket book entries, police and forensic lab memos, forensic examination records and trial and appeal transcripts

As already mentioned there is still a lot of evidence being withheld by Essex

police that we are trying to obtain –
so far with no luck. You must question
when they are convinced they have a
strong and safe conviction what their
reasons are for not handing over these
vital pieces of evidence and information
to us

ROUGH JUSTICE

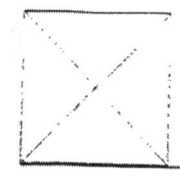

www.jeremybamber.

LIE DETECTOR TEST QUESTIONS, ANSWERS AND RESULTS

19 April 2007

JEREMY BAMBER IS INNOCENT

1. Did you shoot your family on August 7, 1985?   NO
2. Did you shoot five members of your family with an Anschutz rifle?   NO
3. Were you present inside the house when your family was shot with an Anschutz rifle?   NO
4. Did you shoot your father Neville?   NO
5. Did you shoot your mother June?   NO
6. Did you shoot your sister Sheila Caffell?   NO
7. Did you shoot your twin nephews Daniel and Nicholas?   NO
8. Did you hide a rifle silencer in a cupboard after shooting your family?   NO
9. Did you climb out of a window of your parent's home after shooting them?   NO
10. Did you shoot your family in your father's home?   NO
11. Did PC Bews radio in a report of seeing someone in an upstairs window around 4am on the morning of the shooting?   YES
12. Did you pay a professional hit man to shoot your family?   NO

These twelve questions were the subject of the polygraph test taken by Jeremy today. The test was performed by Terry Mullins, member of the American Polygraph Association, BEPA member and British Polygraph Association member who has confirmed that Jeremy is telling the truth. **He has conclusively passed the lie detector test** which he has been asking permission to take since 1991 which until now had been refused.

Police for over an hour and half

The police did not disclose at trial that they could alibi Jeremy, documents establishing this came to light after the failed appeal in 2002.
An entry in the radio monitoring log states that the police were in conversation with someone from inside the house. This was two hours prior to them entering the premises and some hours after Jeremy had police with him. Evidence radio logs

Two police officers and Jeremy had seen someone walk in front of the bedroom window

This verified the fact that two police officers had seen someone walking in front of an upstairs window, confirmed by Jeremy when they were watching the house soon after their arrival. A report of this sighting was sent to headquarters by police radio but has never been disclosed and was later dismissed as 'shadows' – this begs the question of what caused those 'shadows'?

All radio messages were logged by hand and recorded on audio tape. The radio logs made available to the court appear to have been edited and rewritten. Access to these audio recordings would reveal the truth of this but Essex police refuse to hand them over for analysis.

The Essex coroner was provided with evidence sufficient for him to allow the release of the bodies for burial and cremation. The police had informed him that the investigation was ongoing but on the basis of four murders and a suicide. The documents and evidence to substantiate this were lost as were the coroner's files and records – where are the duplicate copies?
Freedom Of Information Act Ombudsman still trying to obtain police pocket books from Essex police, so far without success.

A male and a female body was seen in the kitchen prior to the police entering the house and identified by different police officers after entry was made to the kitchen.

Prior to entering the house two police officers looked into the kitchen through the window and identified a female body. On entering the house the raid team discovered a male and a female body in the kitchen and three further bodies upstairs – all were assumed to be deceased.

There was an operator monitoring a telephone which was off the hook in the kitchen. This was also being recorded. As the police entered the kitchen voices and movement could be heard and this was written in the log. The audio recording is being withheld by Essex police. It would reveal what was being said by whom and why. This is important because at 7.30am there was a male and a female body in the kitchen yet when the crime scene photographs were taken later the female body had disappeared from the kitchen and appeared in the main bedroom with just the male being photographed downstairs in the kitchen. <u>Evidence: communication logs and excerpts from statement of APS John Manners</u>

The kitchen telephone was used by Chief Superintendent Harris prior to the crime scene photographs being taken or any forensic examination of the phone

In 2002 the appal judges were told by the police that the kitchen telephone had not been touched or moved prior to the crime scene photographs being taken. The radio and telephone logs prove that in fact Chief Superintendent Harris used this phone to contact Deputy Chief Constable Simpson. Thereby destroying fingerprints and other evidence and causing the crime scene photographs to be compromised.

A crime scene video was taken by the police of the inside of the house, Dictaphones were also used by investigating officers as they examined the house. The video tape and the audio tapes made that morning are still being withheld by Essex Police. **Freedom Of Information Act Ombudsman still trying to obtain this evidence from Essex police, so far without success.**

Sheila's feet can be seen to be blood stained in previously undisclosed photographs

The courts have always been told that Sheila's feet were spotlessly clean. No photographs were available to the jury showing the soles of her feet. The pathologist gave evidence that the soles of her feet were clean yet photographs now available show the soles of her feet revealing them to be blood stained. **Photographic evidence cannot be shown on this site.**

The pathologist wrote in his hand written pathology notes that Sheila's hands were blood stained yet left this out of his witness statement and the trial evidence telling the court her hands were clean.

The pathologist also told the jury and the court that Sheila's hands were clean and stated this in his witness statement. Why it was edited out that her hands were blood stained as documented in his hand written autopsy notes is not known. Evidence: extract from hand written post-mortem notes

No time of death analysis has been disclosed

It has always been standard practice for a pathologist to take a core body temperature and assess the stage of rigor mortis in order to ascertain and approximate time of death – it is common knowledge that procedure is time, place and cause of death yet if indeed these procedures were followed the finding on the time of death have never been made available or given to the court.

Defence wounds on Mr. and Mrs Bamber show deep fingernail scratch marks. These can be seen on photographs which were again undisclosed to the jury and yet the pathologist makes no mention of them.

Defence wounds on both Mr. and Mrs Bamber show fingernail scratch marks made by someone with long fingernails. The crown's pathologist made no mention of these injuries in his autopsy report or trail evidence. It was only when the undisclosed photographs were looked at that these could be clearly seen. Why were Sheila's long fingernails not scraped for samples? Jeremy's hands and fingernails were scrutinised and found to be clean and his fingernails short. **Photographic evidence cannot be shown on this site.**

Sheila's wounds were still bleeding when she was photographed estimating her death to be at least 3 hours after Jeremy has an accepted alibi, being with the police.

Crime scene photographs show that's Sheila's wounds were still bleeding at the time of the photographing. This puts her time of death no earlier than 7am, at least three hours after Jeremy has been outside with the police. <u>Evidence: excerpts from statement of APS John Manner </u>also see photo 28/07/05 on http://www.studiolegaleinternazionale.com/bamber.php4

Sheila's body was restaged by the police prior to the taking of the crime scene photographs. The police had removed the rifle and then replaced it giving a false impression of the crime scene.

At the 2002 appeal the crown wanted to introduce evidence that Sheila's body was moved after her death in order to prove she was murdered. What the crown did not inform the court and the defence did not discover until later was that prior to the crime scene photographs being taken Essex police had removed the rifle from her body, standing it against the bedroom window frame. It was photographed in this position prior to it being photographed on her body. This is confirmed by a police officer stationed outside in an unused statement where she states seeing what appeared to be a rifle in the window over an hour before any crime scene photographs were taken.

Later when the photographs were taken of Sheila the rifle was replaced on her body and her hands positioned by police officers who used a bible to prop up one arm in order to keep it in position for the photographs. This gave a wholly false photographic record of the scene.

A note consistent with a suicide note recovered by the police along with the bible found on Sheila was kept out of the evidence chain.

On studying the crime scene photographs of the bible found open on Sheila's body it can be seen that a highly relevant hand written note is sticking out from between the pages of the bible. The parts which can clearly be read on enlarging the photographs are highly consistent with a suicide note. There is no record of this note. The police have kept it out of the evidence and it has never been disclosed to neither the prosecution nor the defence. **Photographic evidence cannot be shown on this site.**

Essex police told the appeal court that apart from two stools nothing was touched or moved in the kitchen. Photographs taken prove that two kitchen chairs were moved against the kitchen door prior to the crime scene photographs being taken. Only a policeman could have done this.

On rechecking photographs of the kitchen it can be seen that chairs have been placed in front of the door the police entered through. At the 2002 appeal the judges thought this confusing and dismissed it as photographic foreshortening. The raid team police swore statements saying they did not move these chairs but how could they have entered the kitchen if the chairs were already there? Examination of enlarged photographs show the chairs were so close to the kitchen door as to make it impossible to gain entry and so they must have been moved after the police came in.

The personal pocket books of all the police officers who entered the house that morning have been applied for but Essex police have refused to make these available to the defence or the Freedom of Information Ombudsman. **Photographic evidence cannot be shown on this site.**

Two sound moderators for the .22 rifle were recovered from the house – not by police but by prosecution witnesses. These were given to the police, one on the12th August 1985 and one on the 11th September 1985.

A prosecution witness handed one to the police on the 12th August 1985 and handed the other one to them on the 11th September 1985. Both sound moderators were the same make and model. The first one was taken to a forensic laboratory and examined and taken away the same day for finger printing. During this finger printing process the sound moderator was dismantled, examined and photographed. It was given a forensic reference number and exhibit label. Evidence: excerpts from police action reports.

Prior to these witnesses handling one of the sound moderators to the police they admit in their statement to using a razor blade to remove what they believe to be a flake of blood from one end and trying to dismantle it. Evidence: excerpts from cross examination of Peter Eaton and statement of David Boutflour.

Forensic documents, witness statements and police logs were altered to give the impression that only one sound moderator was recovered from White House Farm when in fact two were discovered.

After the second sound moderator was given to the police it was given a different exhibit label and submitted to the same forensic laboratory for examination. Sometime later it was decided by Essex police to tell the forensic lab both sound moderators were one and the same and could they alter their records to show this. The prosecution witnesses left out of their witness statements and trial evidence that they had submitted two sound moderators to the police and not one as sworn in evidence.

All of the above can be proven and substantiated by reference to previously un disclosed crime scene logs, photographs, witness statements, radio and telephone logs and pocket book entries, police and forensic lad memos, forensic examination records and trial and appeal transcripts.

As already mentioned there is still a lot of evidence being withheld by Essex police that we are trying to obtain – so far with no luck. You must question when they are convinced they have a strong and safe conviction what their reasons are for not handing over these vital pieces of evidence and information to us.

4 supporters online
Jeremy Bamber 2007

A Final Word

VISUALISATION IS EVERYTHING

Visualisation contains creativity without visualisation a tree would remain a tree, instead of becoming the source of wood. It is common knowledge that wood has many by products. Yet without the gift of visualisation and creativity it may well have still remained a tree. It is a well known fact if you put your arms as far as they can stretch around a tree that is a healthy vibrant tree you will feel and also benefit from the energy of the tree. It may not be apparant on your first effort but if you do this regularly you will feel the result. Trees are a living energy. Now I want you to sit quiet, quieten your mind, close your eyes completely relax. I want you to imagine a large plank of wood about 3 metres long by about 12 inches wide. I want you to visualise yourself walking along this plank of wood, first one way and then the other way. The plank of wood is similar to what builders use on the scaffold. Relax even deeper now imagine and visualise the plank of wood one metre off the ground, now do the same again, walk the plank first one way then the other. Some people will have no problem with the change of the plank of wood but a great many will become very hesitant and worried. Why is this so? Well it is because your imagination will show you the negative side and also the possible danger of falling. the secret here is to teach yourself to be confident in your visualisation. Your strength will come from your belief of visualisation.

PREFERANCE

The greatest preferance to life is the needs and not the wants. Life is for the needy and not the greedy. Cultivation will not take place unless the seeds of thought are cultivated to the needs. If you bring happiness to the greatest numbers then results will be noticed. Pleasure without pain cannot be sustained. Pain is not always paramount to ones living, I believe security is the roots of living, from these roots springs forth the fruits of life, success or failure. It is the results of your roots which should be fed with positive constructive elementary belief of a structure rise in your standard of living on a day to day basis which should lead to a better standard of living. There should be no going back. The route to a better future is belief in a better living. People who earn large salaries and end up with very good pensions do so because that is what they chose to do,. It was their decision very few people who retire from work have a suitable pension which they can live comfortably on. Yet most people work for forty years of their lives. So the adice here is make provisions for when you retire. People are living longer now, shortly state pensions could well be a thing of the past. life without provision can be traumatic. The world does not owe you a living as the scout master teaches, be prepared coming events cast their shadows first be prepared,

ROUGH JUSTICE

The first two
Predictions made by
The Virgin Mary
in 1917 turned out to
be correct,and now

The 3rd
Prediction Of Fatima
Is Revealed

The Most terrible secret
of the Vatican
Is now brought To
Light

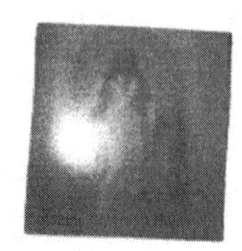

Life in the Raw

I am responsible for my own failures and mistakes.
I am not responsible for other people's inexperience
Or misgivings

Human errors do not find the individual out
What errors do is they reveal the character
Of the person or persons who has made the errors

The thoughts you have in your mind
The feelings you have in your head
The actions of your deeds
Will build the life you desire
No more or less, all can be accomplished
With your own thoughts and fervent desires
Whatever your plans may be
So make sure your thoughts and actions
Work in relation to your ambition
Whatever your dreams may be

I have been to visit many shrines of spiritual significance including Lourdes in France. I have now been guided by visions and direct voices to help any person or persons through absent healing through a private prayer group who send distant healing to the sick, the ill, the afflicted, the possessed or to send healing thoughts to where it is requested.

196

Some time ago I visited Lourdes, in France, where people visit the famous shrine. Millions of people visit this holy shrine where the local girl Bernadette had a vision. At the shrine there is fresh spring water. People are allowed to take containers and bottles of water home with them. On the return journey, going through the Customs check, a Customs Officer asked a lady if she had anything to declare. She replied nothing.

He noticed however that she was carrying large containers and asked her what was in them. She replied holy water from Lourdes. The customs officer took a bottle and removed the top, tasted the contents and said 'this is Brandy'. The woman said 'good God it is a miracle'. I do not wish to offend by this story.

If you give your best then this cannot be bad.

ROUGH JUSTICE

A massive war will kill millions upon millions of people within instants

An Italian journalist has revealed the Best kept secret in religious history. It is the third, last – and by far the most important – prophecy of Fatima. This was the prophecy made by the Virgin Mary in 1917 to three Portuguese Children.

Far from being a prediction of an era of peace and harmony, as may have been hoped, this prophecy warns us of unprecedented catastrophes, and a war that will destroy the planet, raining pain, devastation and death upon almost everyone on it.

The prophecy describes unimaginable horrors, and the Divine retribution that would relegate the Flood to something of minor proportions," said Mario who obtained a copy of the prophecy from a secret Vatican source last May the 3rd.

"It is not surprising that the Vatican has done everything in its power to keep this prophecy secret," continued the Roman newspaperman. "The truth would only cause terror and panic throughout the world. However, as a human being, journalist, and believer, I think that the truth should be revealed."

Despite repeated attempts to get a confirmation, the Vatican has refused all comment on Mario's report.

A spokesperson did, however say privately that: "Schuri knows many people," and would have been quite capable of getting hold of the prophecy, which has been under Vatican lock and key since 1943 – 26 years after the Virgin Mary's appearance to 16-year-old Lucia dos Santos, and her cousins, Jacinta Marto, 8 and Francisco, 9, near the village of Fatima, Portugal, in 1917.

The Vatican Has Officially Confirmed the Appearance Of The Virgin Mary To the Children on several occasions since

---

The Vatican Has Officially Confirmed the Appearance Of The Virgin Mary To The Children on several occasions since

Moreover there is no doubt that two of These prophecies have already been fulfilled

In the first the Virgin Mary stated there Would be a second World War which in Fact occurred from 1939 to 1945. She Also predicted the fall of the Communist Empire

But in the third prophecy it was so horrible That Lucia told no one about it until the Vatican instructed her to write it down And then swore her to secrecy in 1946 The full text, as reported by Schuri appears

The First two Predictions Made by The Virgin Mary In 1917 turned out to be Correct and now,

The 3rd Prediction of Fatima Is Revealed. The most Terrible Secret of the Vatican is now brought to Light

This information was sent to me from a catholic priest who I helped, when I visited the Holy Shrine of Our Lady in Lourdes France.

Here is the full text of the third prophecy given at the village of Fatima:

- "In the near future, although the exact date is not known, humanity will be struck by a major catastrophe. Order and harmony will give way to chaos and anarchy."
- "There will no longer be a Church, and the Papacy will be destroyed."
- "Satan will reign and forces of evil will envelop the earth."
- "Man will be punished by God, and in ways more severe than by the Biblical Flood. This will be the end of time and the end of ends. The great and mighty will perish, along with the small and weak."
- "There will be a great war. Flames and smoke will fill the sky."
- "The waters of the ocean will become mist, its waves will reach a terrifying height, and it will drown all those who encounter it."
- "Millions will die in a flash."
- "Wherever you look, there will be distress, misery, and ruin, throughout many nations."
- "As the time approaches, the abyss will widen. The good will perish along with the bad, the great with the little, and the princes of the Church with the believers.
- "Death will be present throughout the world, because of the terror and crimes committed by the insane and those who act as Satan's agents and who rule the world."
- "Finally, all those who survive will keep proclaiming the Glory of God, and will serve Him as in the days before the world became corrupted. Once again the Prophet will appear to the eyes of the faithful and a new and cleansed era will begin."

PROPHECY WARNING

The first two Predictions made by The Virgin Mary in 1917 turned out to be correct, and now

The 3rd Prediction Of Fatima Is Revealed

The Most terrible secret of the Vatican Is now brought To Light

---

The Virgin specified, however, that this warning is conditional, and that with faith, a new awareness, and determination, all that has been revealed can be avoided.

The prophecy was heard by Jacinta Marto, his brother Francisco and their cousin Lucia dos Santos.

The appearance of the Virgin Mary to these three children in Fatima, Portugal, has been clearly confirmed by the Vatican.

The Vision In the Tree
Some time ago I was very disturbed with various psychic happenings these events made me seek professional help from both the Catholic Church. Plus the Church of England. I also sought help from the spiritual Church. I asked for help and I received help. I had exorcism to relieve me of a spirit that was attached to my psychic mind. During this period of torment I won a holiday to Monte Carlo. This holiday was meant to be? I have a feeling this holiday was sent to me for a purpose. Any way during the holiday I visited many of the famous sites. Plus the Church where Princess Grace of Monaco is laid to rest. After leaving this Church I went along Baden Baden, terrace which is on the new promenade near to the sea. When enjoying the views, I asked my wife to sit on a wall whilst I took a photograph of her. When I was taking the photo I saw a vision of a face,. I mentioned this to my wife, who replied you have had too much red wine, some months later I had the film developed, believe it or not the vision that I had when taking the photograph appeared on the photograph. I was later given several psychic messages regarding future events that will be happening and some have already happened. I am not a goody person I have my failures like everyone else. However I feel the world needs to heed a wake up call for future events. Which will take place.
I enclose a photograph of the vision in the Tree.

The Psychic Path To Wealth, is a motivated collection of ideas to motivate with some effort, a path way to your dreams. The road to success is always under construction. At the crossroads of life it is your own desire that will take you on your journey. To health wealth happiness romance or even failure. The choice is yours entirely.

Instead of day dreaming about your, Un-employment cheque get off your Butt and salvage your Future.
Turn your tears into happiness
Thought Effort Action Results Satisfaction, TEARS
Get the message?

ROUGH JUSTICE

The once very important Town of Coggeshall. In Essex, England

Is not all about antiques and Murders, there is a great charm and a history not far away in the village of Messing. History of the family tree of The American presidents of America. Bush family have been found and recorded.

Coggeshall's unique charm.

Rough Justice
What is it that makes people want to kill fellow humans? Murder at the moment in the Suffolk area of Ipswich in the United Kingdom has been awakened and shocked by the five murders of five different women.
Five prostitutes who worked and walked on the streets of an English Country town. By the very nature of the work these women who sell their bodies for money is extremely dangerous. The fact that they were prepared to jump in to a strangers car for sex several times on any one night of the week only highlights this danger. When some prostitutes often state that the cash to pay for their drug addiction problem. This in itself is problematic because quite often their drug addiction may in time take most of their earnings. Plus if they are unable to pay the drug dealers then many more issues come to light. So all in all it is not all pleasure being a prostitute. However the question at this moment in time is who killed these five prostitutes. The bodies of these five women were all found within a few miles of each other. Two the first two bodies were found naked in a small country river/stream. Another body has been found in woodland. Another two naked bodies have been found in a wooded area of a country road. The joint forces of police officers now have a mammoth job of finding the killer or killers of these five prostitutes. Does history repeat itself? Has the killer killed before? Earlier in my book I have written about The murder of a local doctors wife from Coggeshall in Essex who was found murdered in the Suffolk area over 19 years ago. Many people were questioned yet no one has ever been charged with the murder of Diane Jones. These recent 5 murders of five female prostitutes are unprecedented. The East Anglia town of Ipswich at the moment is in deep shock and disbelief at the publicity that these murders have created. This is not a dress rehearsal. This is the real thing. East Anglia December 2006 is in turmoil. Even the British Prime Minister Tony Blair has openly said that he publicly backs the detectives dealing with this horror that has happened. Many extra police officers from many different counties have been sent to the Ipswich town to help in the much-needed support for the challenging and difficult tack of catching the killer or killers of these 5 prostitutes. One prostitute was interviewed by a reporter and asked why she did what she did for a living; she replied I need the money. When asked about the danger she said she was nervous and accepted the reporters warning that prostitutes have very recently been killed. Just a few days later this same prostitute was also found murdered. The question now

that is the killer, Where does he live? Does he live locally? Some believe he may be using the A14 road or the A12, both roads have easy access to Essex. Coggeshall is only about 20 miles form Ipswich. Diane Jones disappeared in the 1970s and was found in the Suffolk area. Is here murder liked to these fresh? New 5 murders. That have recently taken place in 2006 other women have also been murdered in the surrounding areas over different periods of time, some have never been found. The police have a mammoth task of searching for the clothes, hand bags, mobile phones. And hours of looking at close circuit camera film of the many different aspects of roads, garages, streets and vehicles. The public have also made many thousands of calls to the police incident room. Now it is watch this space. With xmass just over a week to go. It is an awful time for the families of these awful and cruel murders. Their sorrow and disbelief is heartbreaking.

Police information has revealed that one of the Ipswich Rippers victims was 3 months pregnant. The latest report is that a group of around one hundred women, have staged a walk near to the Red light district in Ipswich to reclaim the streets, and quell the fear that has been created by the grim murders of the five ladies of the night.

The Ipswich Ripper?
The news of the world newspaper, is offering a massive £250.000 for the information that will lead to the capture and conviction of the Killer, or killers of these 5 woman Prostitutes, In the Ipswich area, Suffolk.

There are also rumours that a policeman may have been a client of one of the murdered woman

The question now being asked is, Should prostitution be made legal? Should we have sex parlor Brothels? This is a very serious issue indeed. Once the moral Standards of any country fall in to decline, so also will the respect of the nation fall? Beware of short term gains. It may well be the oldest known profession yet it is also, a feed for a need, including money and drugs. The drug culture in the United Kingdom is one of the fastest growing trade, all types of drugs are available in all areas of Village's towns and cities. Even prisons have a drug culture. Crime related drug offences are on the increase. Drug related crime May well lead to more future deaths. Is the killer of these prostitutes a drug user? Does the killer feel prostitutes are an, Easy target to steal their night's earnings? Who knows it is
Watch this space at the moment.

Today the 18th of December a local man from Suffolk who worked in a supermarket has been arrested in relation to the murder of the recent deaths of the five Suffolk prostitutes, it is understood that this arrested man had told a national Sunday newspaper that he knew the entire 5 murdered woman. And that he had been questioned earlier by police. He also is alleged to have stated that he is innocent. A strange story and disbelief indeed, today the 19th of December 2006 a second man from Ipswich has been arrested regarding the murder of the five Ipswich prostitutes?
On the 20th of December 2006 a inquest on the deaths of the 5 Prostitutes was heard and adjourned, what a sensational case this is, 5 murders two arrests all within less than four weeks. The fist suspect after days spent in custody Tom Stevens has been released on police bail. The second suspect Steve Wright has been charged with all five of the Ipswich murders. This man lives in Ipswich near to the red light area from where the woman disappeared. With over 500 police workers from police forces from many parts of the United Kingdom this has been a mammoth operation. A fantastic result

for all the police concerned the deserve a public big Thank you. This case has created interest from all around The world. The deaths of Tania Nicol, Gemma Adams, Anneli Alderton, Paula Clennell and Annette Nichols, will go down in History, they will be remembered for many different things, god bless them may peace be with them. In what their deaths can be only described has Rough Justice for all five of these Ladies of the night.

May there Killer be receive whatever is sanctioned with British Justice, whatever his reasons no one deserves an end Like these 5 Woman suffered. You can fool some people some of the time, you can also fool some people part of the time, yet you cannot fool all the people all of the time, no matter who you are?

A man appeared at Ipswich Court to deist of May, 2007 and was charged with the murder of the five prostitutes murdered in Ipswich, the man pleaded not guilty to all of the murders. The case has been adjourned till January the 14th 2008.watch this space

The case has now been heard, and the accused person has been found guilty of all the five murders. This man has been given life sentences, he has appealed against his convictions, so watch this space.

On the 21.February the jury at Ipswich found Steven White Guilty of the murder of all five women. In the Ipswich area.

On the 23rd of February a full life sentence was passed. This Sentence means that the convicted killer will die in prison, the police are now going to review the deaths of several other murdered women in the East Anglia area the reason I have mentioned these murders is because Steve Wright was initially married in the town of Braintree in Essex. He also lived in Halstead in Essex. Plus he did sometimes drink in the woolpack public house. This was the last place Doctors wife Diane Jones was last seen alive. After leaving this pub in Coggeshall in Essex. Strange But true.

Four Other Women who went missing over the Past Years

Local Doctors wife Diane Jones. Who went missing and was found Murdered In The Suffolk area Inn at Coggeshall inEssex

Also Possible Victims are
Mandy Duncan,
Kellie Pratt, Michelle Bettles, Vicky Hall

It is a Fact, You can tell the truth a thousand times and no one believes you
You can also tell a lie once, and everyone believes you
It's a strange world that we live in today

The Ipswich Prostitute Murders

Steve Wright
The man accused of five prostitutes in the Ipswich prostitutes. Was married in the Essex town of Braintree. He also lived after his marriage in the town of Halstead, plus he often was seen drinking in the local Public House in Coggeshall. The Woolpack. This is the place of the last sightings of the missing Local doctors wife Diane Jones. Who strangely enough was later found murdered somewhere not to fat from Ipswich?

Four other women who went missing over the last 13 years
East Anglia Ripper
Also local Coggeshall Doctors wife Diane Jones, who went missing and was found Murdered in the Suffolk area.

Possible victims include

Mandy Duncan, Vanished, Kellie Pratt, Vanished

Michelle Bettles, Strangled, Vicky Hall, Suffocated

Are these the victim of the East Anglia ,Ipswich, Stalker?

Five Tragic Murders, Five Tragic Deaths, East Anglia Ripper

Five Prostitutes Who have been killed in a Matter of weeks

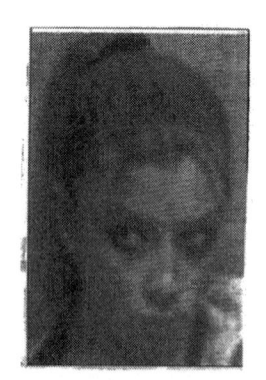

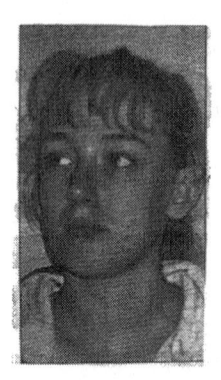

Devil legend

Devil Legend of Tolleshunt Knights

HAVE you ever been told that celebrated tale of the devil and his wicked encounter with a bold knight of old Tolleshunt? It is an ancient legend steeped in Dark Age folklore and mythology and coloured with just a worrying tint of truth. Its origins are mysteriously lost in the dim and distant past and it has obviously been embroided and has developed with the telling but, despite these variations, the plot has always centred on a dispute over the construction of a place called "Barn Hall". Men are said to have started building the hall in a copse of trees, known locally as "devil's wood", in the parish of Virley. When the day's work was done, a brave knight and his three spey bitches were employed to guard the site. During the frightening hours of darkness the man-at-arms was visited by none other than his satanic holiness, the devil. "Who is there?", asked the prince of darkness, and the knight very carefully replied "God and myself and my three spey bitches" and the devil disappeared. Exactly the same thing happened the following evening, satan arrived after the builders had left and asked the knight the same question. Again he cautiously responded "God and myself and my three spey bitches" and a very disgruntled demon flittered away. On the third occasion, however, the champion made a fatal mistake and, when addressed by the devil, answered in the wrong order saying "it is myself and my three spey bitches and God".

Without any hesitation Satan opened his bloody claws and ripped out the chivalrous defender's heart and said he would also have the man's soul "whether buried in church or churchyard". He then picked up a mighty beam from the shell of Barn Hall and threw it onto nearby Tolleshunt Knights with the curse "where this beam shall fall, there shall ye build Barn Hall".

There is still a Barn Hall in Tolleshunt Knights today. The name is said to be a modern form of Saxon "Borooldituna", the place is also mentioned in the mighty Domesday Survey of 1085/86 and about 200 years ago the remains of a Roman villa were found near the house.

But what of the knight I hear you say? Well, his body was apparently taken to "Bushes", or Tolleshunt Knights church and buried in the wall to thwart the devil's curse.

I visited that curious little church the other day, although it is now technically redundant, it has been vested in the Greek Orthodox Religion. Having been given a warm and friendly welcome by the present occupiers, I was shown the interior of this Early English building and immediately noticed the defaced stone effigy of a knight in armour in a niche in the north wall. Said to be the tomb of Sir John atte Lee, who died in c1380, the figure originally held the image of a heart in its cold and rigid hands. Which is a bit strange when you come to think of it.

Arthur Findlay College

The Arthur Findlay College. is situated in Stan stead Mountfitchet.right next Door to Stansted airport.The locals call it Spooks Hall,because of the very nature Of spiritualism plus mediumship and other various groups.the college is a spin off I believe from the author and spiritualist Arthur Findlay.He often has a mental telepathy Conversation with me, on one occasion when I stayed at the college,during the night he Woke me up throwing items about my bedroom.i asked him what was wrong,he said the College was going to downgrade his books,plus employ a top sales director and sell new Age materials like crystals beads and new age stuff.he told the sales manager would not Last very long.believe me this was true.I was so distressed by what he told me,that I cut Short my stay and returned home earlier than expected.i was amazed some time later When I was told the new sales director had been tragically hurt in a car accident near to The Arthur Findlay College. Believe it or not Arthur Findlay Had is a book published here In Tiptree where I now live. IF this is not an Oman than nothing is.

NATURE

Psychic happenings, no matter how alarming and unreal are difficult to understand and even more difficult to understand is why they do occur. The important thing is time. Time is the epitaph of all things. If you live long enough you will see all. Time unfolds all its secrets and mysteries. The passage of time is slow but sure. Not a step forward or a step back will change it. Only the becoming of seasons will fulfil its thirst, a thirst which is difficult to quench or understand its motives.

Time is the master of all what the world entails. The moral of this book is stop worrying about the things you have not got and enjoy the things that you have.

Peter T Healey 6/3/20010
15 Bull Lane. 01621-816921
Tiptree
Colchester
Essex. pthmidas@aol.com
CO OBE Ref Appeal Info

Hi Jeremy

Thank you for your reply to my letter. I have followed your case from the very start.
My info is I feel important. I wrote to the Pope Mrs Thatcher Two MP.S. the home secretary
Chief of Essex Police. My info came about whilst I was employed as a driver handy man
For the Essex county council's was mainly based in Braintree and worked from Coggeshall.
During this time Diana Jones disappeared and was found murdered in Suffolk. Also the antique
Dealer Mr Bull Shot His wife. Also the Braintree Barn murder. then Diana Jones disappeared
local farmer Jimmy Bell acted very stange. he was sent to prison for assaulting his wife. Who he accused
Of having affairs. One day I was parked in a Coggeshall Stoneham street car park. I was sitting in
A ford transit bus. When I heard a commotion. Something was thrown from at a four-wheel drive
Vehicle that was parked next to me. The items hit my vehicle. When I had a look at what was
happening. I saw Jimmy Bell standing outside holding a rifle which had a silencer fitted to the
Rifle. I heard Jimmy Bell Say that next time the Bullets would come from the gun and not the box
That he had thrown at the vehicle. The people inside of the four wheel drive where Mr + Mrs
Bamber. jimmy Bell was saying that mr Bamber had let him down. Mr Bamber quietened Jimmy
Bell and he told me not to be worried. However I did have later confrontations with Jimmy
Bell at his bungalow, which he let out to a couple, whose children I used to take to school
This is part of a book which I have written titled Rough justice do hope this info helps. I was
wandering did the silencer that was found that you mention registered with Mr Bell or Mr
Bamber. if so you may find more info. sometimes the gun and silencer numbers are recorded
God bless I well pray for your release

Kind regards

Peter T Healey CPH

ROUGH JUSTICE

Peter T Healey   1/2/11
15 Bull Lane   01621-816921
Tiptree
Colchester   pthmidas@aol.com
Essex
CO5 0BE   Ref.Appeal

Hi Jeremy.
You are the talk of the washhouse in Essex. Not a bad result so far.
A decision in Principle has been reached. This I feel is a good result.
Because I feel you may well get a retrial. Which would suit your case
Better than three government law lords making a decision.
My advice to you is stop this business of blaming your sister and concentrate
On the fact that you did not commit these mureders.because other wise you
Are conflicting the case. Because if you continue along these lines. And the
Prosecution can prove your sister did not kill the family. Then you will be back
To where you started. I am a spiritalist.and I have a guide who was an author
When he lived in this dimension. He told me if you are cleared on a retrial. Because
Twenty-two years ago I wrote to the Pope John Paul the 11.and asked him to intercede
For you. He sent a reply saying that he would pray for you. The point is now that
Pope John Paul has died. If you are set free. This would be viewed as a miracle. And as I
Have the Pope John 11 reply to my request for him to intercede for you. This could be put
Before the Vatican and if agreed then Pope John the11 could be canonised and have the
Beatification and become A Saint. If so your name would be immortalised in History

I also will pray for you
Best wishis for your review.you can buy me a pint in the ship in Tiptree
When you are released.

Kind regards

Peter T Healey

A Very Strange Coincidence

Several Years Ago an estate agent Susan Lamplouh went missing and was later found murdered, a huge search took place yet no one has been found for her death, however it has been stated that at one time she worked as a stewardess on ships. What also I have discovered was at the time of her disappearance an E fit male was publicised of a Mr. Kipper. It may seem coincidence, but the man recently found guilty of the 6 prostitutes in Suffolk bears a great resemblance to the E fit of Mr. Kipper. He was married in Braintree. He lived in Halstead Essex. And frequently used the woolpack in Coggeshall Essex for a drink. This is the pub where Doctors wife Diane Jones was also found Murdered in Suffolk?Did The Ipswich Ripper.Kill more than the Ipswich prostitutes?.May be he Did

As can be seen with the many documents and letters, this is a very complex case. Some people help some people hinder any investigation.

I received no reply from MP George Galloway to my letter and Soft Disc.

However I did receive a phone call from MP Norman Hunter from the House of Commons.

I wrote to His holiness the pope. I also wrote To Margaret Thatcher When she was Prime Minister concerning my belief that Jeremy Bamber was innocent of these murders which he was found guilty of? And sentenced to life in prison.

I also received a letter from Father David from Coggeshall St Peters Church. He was a great help to me, when things got difficult. Had to have exorcism, because I was being bombarded with Psychic messages from the other side.

However I am still trying to have some break through with my evidence, which should have been heard by the jury at Jeremy Bambers Trial.

If you do not believe there is life after death then. You are lucky indeed. Because if you had witnessed what I have seen and heard for some time. Then you would soon change you Mind?

Before 7 Pints Of Beer.

Health-Warning

Turn the page upside down

After 7 Pints of Beer

The purpose of this book is not to make any money from it being published. The book is because I feel an innocent man is serving a life sentence for a crime that he did not commit.
Not only justice must be done. It has got to also be seen to be done.

Any money from this book will be given to Community watchdog.org.uk

It costs lots of money to help innocent victims of crime.
Donations will be kindly accepted.

Coggeshall's unique charm.

ROUGH JUSTICE

Dear Peter

I have transferred the info into word document and attached in 3 separate lots so you can download and print off what you want - hope this helps.

Best wishes

Some of the information printed in this book. may be from Jeremy Bambers, Web Site
Any proceeds from this book, will be donated free to,
United Faith Healing Foundation.
By the Author.

THE KEY TO HEALTH

A great gift of Healing is yours to find,
If you will penetrate your thoughts inside your mind,
Into the hidden secret depths of solitude and rest,
There will you find sanctuary of the Blest.

I know the feelings of the troubled soul,
Who seeks to find peace of mind where troubles flow,
Yet there in the mind, If you care to control,
Is the greatest gift for miricles yet, to Unfold.

Inside the mind are messages divine,
and gifts untold are yours to find,
Mysterious Healing Powers are within Oneself,
But only you yourself can unlock the gift and set yourself free,
Yes only you yourself possess the key,
The Key to unlock your mind.

Peter T. Healey

THE LOST CLUES THAT COULD CLEAR THE Bamber's KILLER

I wish to offer my full apology to any family and friends of the deceased.
This was not by any means a straight forward case, many mistakes have been made. I feel justified in bringing this evidence to the proper authorities, a man is serving a life sentence for crimes I feel he has not committed. He has passed a lie detector test after many years spent in prison.
It would have a sensible idea to give the same treatment to his girlfriend and let the public see was she telling the truth. Once again I make a full apology for once again for renewing this dreadful case.

Author

A Very Strange Coincidence

Bamber: 'I will die a free man'

Jeremy Bamber has told the EADT that he still believes he will one day walk free from prison, despite being told yesterday he will spend the rest of his life behind bars.

Bamber, serving life for killing five members of his family at their Essex farmhouse in 1985, was told by a judge that the murders were so "exceptionally serious" that he would die in jail.

The killer was originally told he would serve 25 years, before former Home Secretary Michael Howard increased the sentence to his whole natural life.

The 47-year-old, who has always protested his innocence, had hoped to be given a tariff that would give him some hope of parole.

But after reviewing the case, Mr Justice Tugendhat said: "These murders were exceptionally serious.

"In my judgment, you ought to spend the whole of the rest of your life in prison, and I so order."

The judge said he had read submissions from Bamber's solicitors pointing out that he was not suffering from mental illness and was behaving and progressing well in prison.

He had also read victim impact statements from the remaining family members.

Bamber was found guilty by a majority verdict of shooting his wealthy adoptive parents, June and Nevill, his sister Sheila Caffell, and her six-year-old twin sons Daniel and Nicholas at their farmhouse in Tolleshunt D'Arcy, near Maldon.

The prosecution said he had murdered them out of greed, hoping to inherit a £500,000 fortune.

Archives

New Evidence 19/09/04

Mirror Article 21/11/04

Daily Mail 12/01/08

Chronicle 27/01/05

Latest news May 07

East Anglian 16/07/05

4 year summary

News update 19/01/05

East Anglian 6/08/05

The Bible Issue

Freedom of information

Independent 3/08/05

Daily Mail 19/05/07

Mailing List

To be notified when this site is updated and new content is added you can

217

Speaking to the EADT yesterday, Bamber said: "I still believe that I will die a free man.

"But I find it incredible that on the one hand they say this and on the other hand they will have to release me for a retrial.

"I have the evidence that can prove my innocence but it does not make any difference - it seems that they can do what they like.

"The Criminal Cases Review Commission (CCRC) has had years to make its decision on the case."

He claimed: "There are 58 missing photos of the crime scene - the key ones that show Sheila's body was restaged - and they are the ones that have been withdrawn from the file - it is scandalous. We have been asking for them for the past nine months.

"I am prepared to have a retrial, I have done everything I can do get the case reviewed, it is utterly frustrating - I have told the truth since day-one to now, but all they want to do is suppress the evidence."

It has also emerged that Bamber has been barred from corresponding with his legal team after his "rule 39" entitlement was withdrawn.

He claimed: "They do not want to admit the truth of my innocence - it is a form of mental torture - 'get the few last kicks in before we have to let him go'.

"I believe the prison governor will have to backtrack and say 'no we can't do that', but I now have a gagging order on me and it will take four or five months to remove it through the courts.

"In the end the truth will come out.

"The information is out there now - they can't put it back in the box - it is in the public arena now."

Bamber's solicitor Marcus Farrar said: "We were hoping that there would be at least some prospect of knowing when he could be released, but to have no light at the end of the tunnel is a disappointment to him."

He said there could be an appeal against the decision in the British courts, but did not rule out taking the case to the Europe.

And on the "missing" photos, he said: "There has been no reason given for the non-disclosure of the photos. They are in existence as the CCRC has them, but their stance is they seem to send us the ones they think we need and are considering the request for the other ones.

"We don't know what is on them, but would like to see them so we can see one way or the other if they are of assistance to us."

David Boutflour, Bamber's cousin, said: "We were anxious as to what the outcome might be - you have to remember that what he did and what he has the potential to do.

"We now have a sense that justice and common sense has prevailed - it had been a worrying situation.

"I have family and a grandchild now and safeguarding them is paramount and we worry what would happen if he did come out.

"I am saddened that he will have to spend the rest of his life in prison, but for everybody's security, I think that is the only place he can remain."

A spokeswoman for the CCRC said they could not discuss the details of the missing photos.

She said: We are unable to say very much about this - just that the case is still under review and it is taking this amount of time because of the complexities of the case."

She said there was no indication about when the decision would be taken about referring the case to the Court of Appeal.

An Essex Police spokeswoman said they could not comment on the case because of the ongoing CCRC review.

A Home Office spokeswoman said they could not comment on individual prisoners.

1 supporter online

The Bamber murders where happenings of a much bigger
Picture of the events that where taking place in Essex at
The time. When some very serious events took place
People seem to think that they know everything
Yet they fail to understand what they do know.
I am not saying Jeremy Bamber Should Be Freed.
What I am suggesting is that he was entitled to a fair
Trial. I feel the prosecution service have withheld certain
Crucial evidence in the Jeremy Bamber court case. It would
Seem fair to close this case and settle the facts legally
Many people hide behind a cloak of respectability, yet
If their lives where open to be viewed. You would find some
Are as devious has sewer rats.
Author.

Surprising that greed is a big player in lives. A prosperous persons cup is never full neither is a devious persons need.

Life's journey is unpredictable. Is death the end of a problem? Or just an insight in to more dilemmas, ask a dead man he may tell you or are we freaks of computerization. DNA the modern identity sheds no light on this subject, it just adds to the fact, that computerization plays, more than a big part in life. The 4 seasons tell you this, the tides that turn, the sun and moon that shines, they may well be driven by a computer time clock? Life mystery will no doubt unfold its secrets, the designer of this universe did not leave a road going nowhere, so enjoy the journey, and the challenge. I ask this because life is not always fair. There is a dark side to nature as the tale of Jeremy Bamber unfolds. If you are in the wrong place at the wrong time, Life can be unjust.

An interesting fact about Coggeshall, just a few miles away less than 10 minutes, lies the Hamlet of Messing. Many years ago this was the Ancestral home of The Bush family, whose descendants George w Bush.

And his father became Presidents Of America. A little further on is the Village of Tolleshunt Knights where there is a very small church named Bushes Church? Who knows what roads our journey will lead us to.

Killer Bamber gets more time to reply to rejection of appeal

KILLER Jeremy Bamber has been given longer to respond to a provisional decision to reject his latest appeal.

Bamber, pictured, has been in jail for more than 24 years after he was found guilty of shooting his adoptive parents, June and Nevill, sister Sheila Caffell and her six-year-old twin sons, Daniel and Nicholas, at their farmhouse in Tolleshunt D'arcy in 1985.

He has always claimed Mrs Caffell shot the family before shooting herself.

The Criminal Cases Review Commission made a provisional decision not to refer his murder convictions to the Court of Appeal earlier this year.

Bamber has been told the commission is not yet in a position to reach a decision and has extended the time in which he needs to respond to their provisional decision.

A spokesman for the commission said: "Mr Bamber and his team have requested a further two months to make further submissions.

"The commission has extended the time limit for submissions until July 22.

"The matters being discussed have included questions about the disclosure of crime scene photographs and negatives."

Seen to be done

I could hardly believe what I was reading in the latest issue of the Tribune concerning the Jeremy Bamber murder trial.

There is no doubt that this is one of the very worst miscarriages of justice that has been allowed to stand, and all because of neglectful and unlawful conduct by Essex Police. I think that the editor should be applauded for bringing such news to the attention of local residents.

Not only should justice be done, justice should be seen to be done, and I feel that our member of parliament Priti Patel should use her experience and position to ask questions in the house for the prime minister to answer.

Peter Healey
Bull Lane, Tiptree

Acknowledgements

I must mention my wife Joan who has kept me sane over the past 35 years with help and guidance and lots of patience. She has made me a much better person. So I say to my wife you are simply the Best.

I must remember Arthur Findlay. Who has sent messages and instructed me over many issues.
He even made himself visible to me. He used to have his books on spiritualism published in Tiptree Essex. He also was the founder of (Spooks hall) this is what locals call The Beautiful Arthur Findlay College. He believes new age criteria and new laws to supposed to protect people from fraud mediums. Is just a get out to stem the interest in the movement?
Not to believe in life after death is not to believe you are conceived through your mother. Life is a journey. Who would set out on such an event? And not believe he is going somewhere.

The creator of the universe never made. The road to nowhere. It life has its purpose. So have faith. And your journey will be revealed soon enough.

Also Gordon Higginson a past president of the spiritual movement has also made himself very useful to me with comfort and reassurance and support, I say to him thank you.

Peter T Healey

Spiritual Coggeshall Essex

What can I add to my memories of this quaint?
English Dwelling except that it helps change My Life. In the Woolpack Inn is a living Spirit of a woman called Sarah Hinchcliff. She told me she was originally from Yorkshire? And she was an early healer. She could tell of future happenings. However some Gentry believed that she was a witch. She was later dipped in the river in Coggeshall, and then burned in the Market Place in Coggeshall. One other point is that the convicted Murderer of the 6 Ipswich Prostitutes used to drink in the Woolpack Inn in Coggeshall.
Why not visit Coggeshall, and the Church, and see the carved Wooden Madonna.

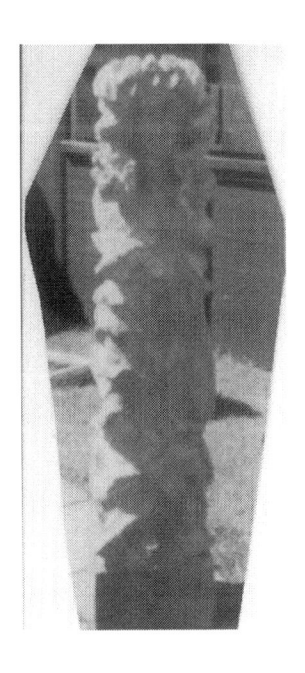

ROUGH JUSTICE

Home

About Mr Healey

Faith Healing

Mind Power

A Final Word

Final Word

THE KEY TO HEALTH

A great gift of Healing is yours to find,
If you will penetrate your thoughts inside your mind,
Into the hidden secret depths of solitude and rest,
There will you find sanctuary of the Blest.

I know the feelings of the troubled soul,
Who seeks to find peace of mind where troubles flow,
Yet there in the mind, if you care to control,
Is the greatest gift for miracles yet, to unfold.

Inside the mind are messages divine,
and gifts untold are yours to find,
Mysterious Healing Powers are within Oneself,
But only you yourself can unlock the gift and set yourself free,
Yes only you yourself possess the key,
The key to unlock your mind.

Peter T. Healey

LINKS

United Faith Healing Foundation

I have been to visit many shrines of spiritual significance including Lourdes in France. I have now been guided by visions and direct voices to help any person or persons through absent healing through a private prayer group who send distant healing to the sick, the ill, the afflicted, the possessed or to send healing thoughts to where it is requested.

2/2/11 03 FEB 2011   JEREMY BAMBER
                           A5352AC
                           HM FULL SUTTON
                           YORK
                                YO41 1PS

DEAR PETER,
 THANK YOU FOR YOUR LETTER.
YOU RAISE AN INTERESTING POINT
WITH REGARDS TO THE DEFENCE
POSITION OVER SHEILA BEING
RESPONSIBLE.
 HOWEVER YOU HAVE TO APPRECIATE
THAT OUR LEGAL POSITION DOES
NOT INCLUDE ANYTHING ABOUT
SHEILA — THAT IS NOT NECESSARY.
BUT THE MEDIA DO NOT WORK
LIKE THE COURTS, THEY DO NEED
TO KNOW, "WELL IF ITS NOT
YOU WHO DID COMMIT THE
MURDERS?" — ITS NOT ENOUGH
TO SAY "I DON'T KNOW." SO
I SIMPLY PRESENT ALL THE ACTUAL
EVIDENCE FROM THE CASE PAPERS.
 PLUS A MISTAKE YOU'VE MADE
IS THAT THE PROSECUTION HAVE ANY
INPUT INTO AN APPEAL — THEY
CANNOT RAISE ANY ISSUE THAT
WASN'T PART OF THEIR CASE AT
MY TRIAL — UNLESS ITS SOMETHING
LIKE DNA EVIDENCE AND ONLY THEN
WITH PERMISSION CAN IT BE INTRODUCED.
 IT IS KIND OF YOU TO WORRY
ABOUT ME, AND PERHAPS JOHN PAUL II

> MIGHT ASSIST, BUT COULD MY BEING
> GIVEN JUSTICE REALLY BE SEEN AS A
> MIRACLE - I DON'T THINK SO.
>   I LOOK FORWARD TO HAVING A DRINK
> WITH YOU IN THE SHIP ONE DAY
> SOON
>   WITH EVERY GOOD WISH

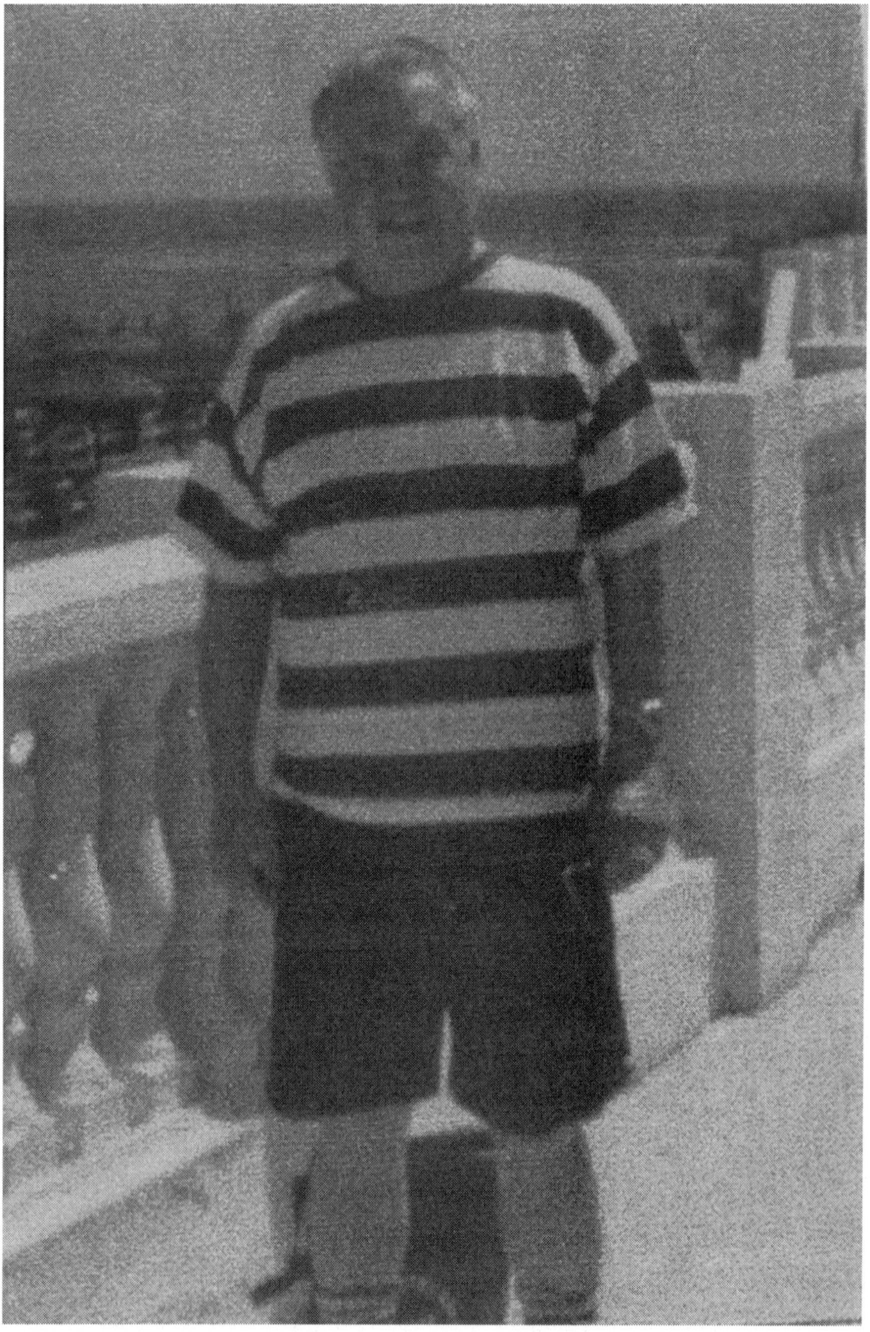

The Woolpack inn. Coggeshall
The last place Diane Jones was
Seen alive?

Coggeshall Famous Characters

At the time of these events that are mentioned one more sticks in my mind. The Famous London film star Michael Caine, became a business partner with a Mr. Peter Langham they opened a brassier cum restraint in Coggeshall Peter Langham was a great character. He could lighten up a coal mine with his personality. At the time Coggeshall had 30 antiques shops. So it can be seen it attracted a great many Diverse customers. Even gangsters form the London area. It came as a great shock to many people when the news came that Peter Langham had died. Apparently somehow he set fire to himself. There was so much evil in the area you could feel the aura of the town change with doubt anxiety and unbelief in the many happenings that took place. It is now back to normality and is well worth a visit. Peace has been restored again. But no doubt people will talk about these times until the end of the World.

Auras.Karma.Vibes.Negativity

What a subject to play around with. I asked many residents what they thought about the happenings in the Coggeshall area. Some had no explanation to offer. Some thought about greed. Some said there was a lay line going through Coggeshall and this may be the answer. But on local old (snout) that seemed to know everything told me. Peter he said. Greed will always find a way. Then he told me. That some time ago a local well to do. Had come across 6 Rhino horns. Which he said were worth a fortune when sold to China. And later ground to powder for medicine. He sold these horns and people made lots of money. Then this well to Gent. Said he had come across 4 more Rhino Horns. By this time there was a great interest in the easy way to make big money. However some of the business people were so eager to make huge profits that they paid in advance for these extra 4 Rhino horns. This was a mistake. Because there were no more Rhino horns. And the seller did a runner with the cash. Leaving some confused angry business men who had just lost a fortune? So you can see why so much evil was in the air.

(This I feel sums it Up)
There is enough in the world for the worlds needs
Yet not enough for the world greed
Yet if everyone cared enough. And everyone shared enough
Then everyone could have enough
Everything on the earth is negative. With positive nature.
Your mind can create positively for all sorts of reasons some
Have it. Some do not have it. Some will some wont. Some can
And some cannot.
Whatever your thoughts on this issue. The fact is your
Thoughts

Create your Karma whether for good or for evil. It is not
What you think you are (But what you think you (are)
One Question Now Remains. Do You Think That Jeremy Bamber.
(Is Innocent)
?

When humans are confronted with lives. Origin, and the question arises where did we come from. Where will we go? It is not totally surprising that greed is a big player in lives. A prosperous persons cup is never full. Neither is a devious persons need.

Life's journey is unpredictable. Is death the end of the problem? Or just an insight in to more. Dilemmas ask a dead man he may tell you or are we freaks of computerization. DNA the modern identity sheds no light on this subject. It just adds to the fact that computerization plays more than a big part in life. The 4 seasons tell you this, the tides that turn, the sun and moon that shines, they may well be driven by a computer time clock? Life mystery will no doubt unfold its secrets, the designer of this universe did not leave a road going nowhere, so enjoy the journey, and the challenge. I ask this because life is not always fair. There is a dark side to nature as the tale of Jeremy Bamber unfolds. If you are in the wrong place at the wrong time, Life can be unjust.

An interesting fact about Coggeshall, just a few miles away less than 10 minutes, lies the Hamlet of Messing. Many years ago this was the Ancestral home of The Bush family, whose descendants George w Bush.

And his father became Presidents Of America. A little further on is the Village of Tolleshunt Knights where there is a very small church named Bushes Church? Who knows what roads our journey will lead us to.

Because once your battery has run out. You have little to say on this matter. Except to wait for your life past to be downloaded for a review.

Treat the Tales from the Bible as Stepping-stones form the Past, And Not Your Future. Because without worldwide Justice. The world will hold no
(Future)
I feel the case for Jeremy Bamber is Unjust. He seems too cursed by bad Misfortune. First his girlfriend gave evidence against him. Then the police colluded over various pieces of evidence. On top of that at his trial he was sentenced to 25 years imprisonment, then, the Home secretary Michael Howard, Converted the sentence to Life. Because it was such a nasty case. In all if this was not the case he could now have been a free man. Instead

of being banged up for life. Some of the villains who frequented Essex at the time of these Murders. The Firm. Run with Ronnie + Reggie Kray. Plus brother Charlie Kray. They are all brown Bread now. However the underworld still exists. With people with long memories. The reason I mention this is because the underworld holds grudges against child murderess if Jeremy Bamber is ever released. There will always be people who still believe he may or was guilty? Not a nice situation to be in in between a rock and a hard place. So after reading this book says a prayer for all those, who have felt pain, and sorrow, in these grave ordeals

Last Notes
Jesus said to me, I heard a man praying
In a prison Cell, so I have sent a messenger
The messenger is You Peter

Australian authorities look to send Neale to UK after prison term
Former solicitor faces deportation from Oz

A FORMER high-profile Colchester solicitor is set to be deported back to Britain after he has served a life sentence for drug smuggling.

Jimmy Neale was once a high-profile figure in the town. He played hockey for England, married a beauty queen and lived in luxury in Chitts Hill.

However, he fell from grace when he was found guilty at the Old Bailey of theft and defrauding clients of his law firm in 1985. He was sentenced to three years in prison and was struck off as a lawyer. Then, in 1993, he was found guilty of conspiracy to defraud and was sentenced to a further 18 months in jail.

He moved to Hong Kong in 1997 and, the following year, bought a wine company.

In 2002 he was jailed for life after he was caught smuggling 271,000 ecstasy tablets into Australia in a shipment of French wine.

At the time, the £millions bust was Australia's biggest drugs find. He claimed he had been pressured to smuggle the drugs by triads and said he thought the tablets were Viagra.

Neale, who is now 65, is serving his sentence in the Mid North Coast correctional centre near Sydney, Australia, and is due to be considered for parole in four years.

A spokesman for the New South Wales Corrective Services said: "The Federal Department of Immigration intends to deport him whenever he is released, presumably to the UK.

"James Neale, as a well-behaved prisoner and is currently in the minimum security area."

Neale is appealing for donations to help fight his conviction at his website james.neale.co.uk.

He suffered personal tragedy in 1988, when his schizophrenic son, Jonathan, killed his mother, Neale's ex-wife, Rosemary. Jonathan was convicted of manslaughter due to diminished responsibility and was ordered to be detained indefinitely under the Mental Health Act.

Auras.Karma.Vibes.Negativity

(Freedom of Information)
May Lead to Freedom
(Jeremy-Bamber)

Extra time for Bamber work

LAWYERS for convicted murderer Jeremy Bamber have been given two more months to back up claims trial evidence was fabricated.

Bamber is serving life for shooting five members of his adoptive family at White House Farm, Tolleshunt D'Arcy in 1986.

Scott Lomax, who is pressing for Bamber's release, said his team had been given until September 9 for extra scientific investigations into the original trial evidence. He says scratch marks were made after crime scene photos had been taken.

Mr Lomax said: "The new work uses the latest forensic and analytical techniques – like something from CSI. I have no doubt it will prove with certainty evidence used to convict Jeremy Bamber should not have been used."

Bamber's lawyers were originally given three months to prepare the case to seek a fresh appeal.

Bamber given yet more time

Last week Jeremy Bamber, currently serving a whole of life tariff for murdering five members of his family at a Tolleshunt D'Arcy farmhouse in 1985, was told that the Criminal Cases Review Commission (CCRC) had extended their submissions deadline for a second time. The extension is from 22 July to 9 September and is to allow work to be carried out that had been delayed as a result of the complex and exhaustive permissions process related to the availability of certain photographic images.

Also last week, the European Court of Human Rights confirmed that the closing date for their hearing into the legality of Bamber's whole life tariff would be 15 September. After this date it will be decided whether the sentence will be put back down to 25 years. If the court rules in Bamber's favour he should be eligible for parole, and any application is likely to be viewed favourably and with urgency since he has already served almost 26 years for a crime which he continues to insist that he did not commit.

'I am extremely pleased with the work submitted to the European Court of Human Rights by my legal team', said Bamber 'and I am sure that the illegally imposed whole life tariff will be returned to its original 25 years and I will be eligible for parole. However, I think it unlikely that my freedom will come through this route as I am convinced that my conviction will be overturned before then.

'I have been working late into the night on my case in preparation for further revelations from documents that the defence has never seen before. Many of these were kept from me under the old regulations, but when the Freedom of Information Act came into force it became possible to obtain a number of previously unavailable records.

'Although these new finds have made a huge difference to my case, and I know that my freedom is now very close, there are still documents that are being withheld. I am currently awaiting material from my second freedom of information request, but I anticipate that Essex Police will come up with yet more excuses as to why I cannot have access to documents that provide vital evidence in my case.

'The recent phone hacking scandal has raised questions about the honesty and integrity of many police officers and I am convinced that this sort of corruption and bribery has continued throughout our justice system since at least the 1970s. But I will not be striking any deals and I will not be gagged. The truth will be known and I will continue to speak it freely.'

Final Observations

The Town of Coggeshall has lost another of its characters. Local Farmer Jimmy Bell, has killed himself after first shooting his second wife Augusta. This is the third murder that has taken place, to shock everyone in the town. The shootings happened in the home on Jimmy Bell's wife parents. The child's grandmother left the house during the violent argument. The local police said that they were not looking for anyone else for this crime.

A baby girl was snatched to safety minutes before her father went berserk with a shotgun and blasted her mother to death. Jimmy Bell was a farmer. His life became very odd after he believed his wife had been unfaithful. As a result he was found later to be jailed for six months for assault on his first wife. After serving his sentence Jimmy Bells behaviour became more erratic. Jimmy Bell was also a farmer. Jimmy Bell and Neville Bamber were at one time close friends. However, after blaring row, their friendship seemed to be doomed. I often came across Jimmy Bell several times a week walking the Marks Hall carrying his rifle with a silencer fitted to the rifle. Jimmy Bell was an expert shot. After the Bamber murders, I failed to understand why Jimmy Bell's gun licence were investigated. I believe that the Essex police did not take into account the full picture of what was going on in Coggeshall at the time of the Bamber murders, because there is and was a very strong link to most of these killings.

As I have already stated Jimmy Bells behaviour changed after his spell in prison. One day I released some young racing pigeons in Marks Hall for a gentle training exercise. When the pigeons were airborne, I heard several rifle shots. Jimmy Bell was taking pot shots at my pigeons. To sum my story up, only one person knows if Jeremy Bamber committed the massacre of his adopted family. That person is Jeremy Bamber himself, because of the many great mistakes made by The Essex Police. In this case I feel the least that can be offered is a retrial.

Final Observations

(Back Page)
Do you believe about being in the right place, at the wrong time? If so then continue reading my encounter. For five days a week for eleven years I was based in a small Part of Essex UK, during this period of time. Unbelievable True events took place, there was murder. Murders and murderers, plus witchcraft, homosexuality and Drugs. A popular night club owner's wife was murdered during a robbery. A local doctors wife disappeared and was found murdered. A local farmer was jailed for actual harm to his wife. Then he remarried. And later shot his second wife. Then he killed himself. An Italian Tony killed a well-known London gangster's brother. Then he was murdered. A local landscape gardener murdered a local lady. Yet unbeknown he had already been in jail FOR A SIMILAR offence. So many happenings in a small area. Then in Ipswich several prostitutes were murdered by a man living locally, there was a witchcraft and local coven. So much so that it effected my mind's had to have exorcism, during which I was given messages that became true. There is much more. So read the book. And read for yourself. This strange encounter with the Underworld, of the unknown.
Author

Peter T Healey

This is not the end of the Tales.Just an Insight in to what can happen any where in any Town?

ML0974 QP100664 0904

3/3/10

JEREMY BAMBER
J A5352AC
HM FULL SUTTON
YORK
YO41 1PS

DEAR PETER,
THANK YOU FOR YOUR LETTER WHICH I RECEIVED TODAY. I KNOW THAT YOU HAVE SPOKEN AT LENGTH TO LEE ABOUT ALL THAT YOU HAVE DISCOVERED. OF COURSE I AM MOST GRATEFUL FOR YOUR OFFER, BUT BEFORE I INVOLVE MY VERY BUSY LAWYERS I NEED TO BE SATISFIED MYSELF THAT THE INFORMATION YOU HAVE CAN ADD SOMETHING TO MY APPEAL — SO IF YOU WOULD LIKE TO SEND ME THE MATERIAL YOU FEEL MIGHT ASSIST ME I WILL GLADLY GIVE IT MY FULL ATTENTION AND IF IT ADDS TO OUR GROUNDS OF APPEAL I WILL THEN PASS IT ON TO MY LAWYERS FOR THEIR ATTENTION.
I AM SURE THAT YOU HAVE SEEN THE LATEST DEVELOPMENTS RE MY CASE CONCERNING THE PAINT/SOUND MODERATOR/SCRATCH MARK ISSUE.
WE NOW KNOW THAT ANN EATON AND/OR DAVID BOUTFLOUR TOOK A SOUND MODERATOR FROM MY DADS GUN CUPBOARD AND USED IT TO SCRATCH THE PAINT ON THE

2

UNDER SIDE OF THE MANTLE SHELF IN THE KITCHEN OF WHITE HOUSE FARM — THEY DID THIS IN ORDER TO FRAME ME WITH MURDER SO THEY COULD STEAL MY INHERITANCE SO ANY INFORMATION YOU MIGHT HAVE REGARDING ANN EATON OR DAVID BOUTFLOUR WOULD BE OF THE HIGHEST PRIORITY
I LOOK FORWARD TO READING THE INFORMATION IN YOUR POSSESSION
YOURS SINCERELY
Jeremy Bamber

Bamber claims new evidence of his innocence

CONVICTED killer Jeremy Bamber claims to have new evidence from leading ballistics experts which he says proves his innocence.
Bamber, 33, was jailed in 1986 for the murders of his parents Nevill and June, his sister Sheila Caffell and her twin sons Nicholas and Daniel, at White House Farm, Tolleshunt D'Arcy.
He has consistently protested his innocence.
Now he has submitted a new application to the Criminal Cases Review Commission, which includes evidence from leading ballistics experts in the UK and US which focuses on wounds to Sheila's neck, claiming they were made with a rifle without a sound moderator.
During the trial at Chelmsford Crown Court, the jury was told Bamber's cousin, David Boutflour, had found a silencer in a cupboard three days after the killings.

196

242

In North Yorkshire's Full Sutton maximum security jail, prisoner A5352AC will be getting up as usual at 7.00am to start poring over a huge pile of documents in which he hopes to find the key to his release. He has followed the same routine for the past 26 years, but now Jeremy Bamber's hopes that his whole-life tariff might be coming to an end are looking less fanciful.

His fate rests on the judgement of three legal experts who make up the panel of the Criminal Cases Review Commission (CCRC). They are meeting to evaluate evidence that has been presented to them over the past two years and will shortly decide whether Bamber's case should be referred to the court of appeal for the third time. The material that they will be considering includes documents and statements that were not available, or, as Bamber claims, suppressed by the police and the prosecution at the original trial and in the subsequent appeals. A third referral would raise the possibility that Bamber has been the victim of one of the UK's longest and most damning miscarriages of justice. It would also call into question many aspects of the police investigation and the way that the prosecution case was made.

One of the most significant new pieces of evidence was uncovered during a recent investigation by the *Observer* newspaper. According to Bamber's legal team, it 'shakes the safety of [the] conviction to the core'.

The original view of the police was that Sheila Caffell, Bamber's adoptive sister, had shot her two children and her parents at the family home in Tolleshunt D'Arcy before turning the gun on herself. But this theory was cast into doubt when Bamber's cousin David Boutflour produced a silencer that he claimed to have found in a kitchen cupboard some days after the murders had been committed.

Police forensic reports indicated that traces of blood found on the end of the silencer matched Sheila's blood group, and officers concluded that it would have been impossible for her to shoot herself with the extended barrel and then replace the silencer in a cupboard. This was the pivotal issue that persuaded the jury that Jeremy Bamber must have been responsible for the murders, particularly after the judge instructed them that the silencer 'could, on its own, lead them to believe that Bamber was guilty'.

However, the *Observer* team has obtained evidence suggesting that a silencer was never used at all. According to their report, David Fowler, the chief medical examiner of the US state of Maryland and a veteran of over 3,000 homicide investigations, reviewed photographic evidence of the entry wounds in Sheila Caffell's neck and concluded 'In my professional opinion, the [burn marks] complex ... of the lower entrance and two abrasions is consistent with the rifle not having a silencer'.

Fowler's opinion is supported by independent investigations carried out by Ljubisa Dragovic, chief medical examiner of Oakland county in Michigan, and Marcella Fierro, former chief medical examiner of Virginia. The conclusion was further corroborated by analysis of a burn mark found on Sheila's father Nevill Bamber's back when Oxfordshire-based forensic scientist John Manlove said 'From its size and shape, this mark could possibly have been caused by the hot muzzle of a firearm without a sound moderator'. A subsequent report by Daniel Caruso, chief of burn services at the Arizona Burn Centre and executive chair of the department of surgery at the University of Arizona, stated 'In my professional opinion, the three wounds sustained by [Nevill] Bamber are consistent in size, shape and diameter with a threaded end of a model 525 Anschütz rifle barrel heated sufficiently to cause injury.'

Bamber's solicitor Simon McKay said 'The evidence of three senior and respected pathologists that the wounds to Sheila Caffell are consistent with the rifle having been fired without the silencer fitted shakes the safety of Jeremy Bamber's conviction to the core.

Observer reporters that the original investigation was 'mishandled'. He confirmed that officers who had attended the crime scene later compared notes of the incident, although he rejected any allegations of collusion. 'We sat down together: it was permissible under what was called judges' rules in those days', he said.

Bamber continues to assert that more than 40,000 documents and 211 photographs relating to the case are still being withheld by police, but among those that have been submitted to the CCRC are photographs showing that Sheila's body and the murder weapon were moved by scene-of-crime officers. Essex Police continue to deny that the crime scene was tampered with in any way.

Ex-sergeant Bews, who was one of the first officers to arrive at White House Farm on the night of the murders, studied the pictures and commented 'Somebody has obviously moved her hand. I don't think any of the police involved at the time would disagree that it was a badly handled investigation.'

In a further development, Bamber's cousin David Boutflour, who claimed to have found the silencer in a cupboard, has admitted for the first time that he inherited a significant sum of money from Nevill Bamber's estate. 'I have inherited quite a large amount of money as a result of Jeremy', he said. 'And most of it I've wasted, I've spent.'

Boutflour has consistently maintained that Bamber's is guilty of the murders and he was a key prosecution witness at the trial. But Bamber's supporters have long argued that since Boutflour stood to benefit from his cousin's conviction, this should have been emphasised to the jury before they heard his evidence.

Bamber was described by the trial judge as 'warped and evil beyond belief'. He is one of 38 convicted killers in Britain who have been given a whole-life tariff, meaning that he will never be released. Others include Ian Brady, Donald Neilson, Rosemary West and Peter Tobin. Only Bamber has

Sheila Caffell with her twin sons

Made in the USA
Charleston, SC
13 September 2012